OUTDOOR

PAINT
TECHNIQUES
& FAUX FINISHES

REVISED EDITION

25 Great Outdoor Finishes for Plaster, Wood, Cement, Metal, and Stone

Marina Niven & Louise Hennigs

CREATIVE
HOMEOWNER®

CRE▲TIVE
HOMEOWNER®

Outdoor Paint Techniques & Faux Finishes, Revised Edition
Vice President–Content: Christopher Reggio
Editor: Katie Ocasio
Technical Editor: Chris Cavanaugh
Design: David Fisk
Index: Jay Kreider

ISBN 978-1-58011-814-9

Library of Congress Cataloging-in-Publication Data

Names: Niven, Marina, author. | Hennigs, Louise, author.
Title: Outdoor paint techniques & faux finishes / Marina Niven & Louise
   Hennigs.
Other titles: Outdoor painting techniques & faux finishes | Outdoor paint
   techniques and faux finishes
Description: Revised edition. | Mount Joy : Creative Homeowner, 2018. |
   Includes index.
Identifiers: LCCN 2018031750 (print) | LCCN 2018032526 (ebook) | ISBN
   9781607655312 | ISBN 9781580118149
Subjects: LCSH: House painting--Amateurs' manuals. | Finishes and
   finishing--Amateurs' manuals.
Classification: LCC TT320 (ebook) | LCC TT320 .N58 2018 (print) | DDC
   698/.1--dc23
LC record available at https://lccn.loc.gov/2018031750

We are always looking for talented authors. To submit an idea, please send a brief
inquiry to acquisitions@foxchapelpublishing.com.

Printed in Singapore

Current Printing (last digit)
10 9 8 7 6 5 4 3 2 1

Creative Homeowner®, *www.creativehomeowner.com*, is an imprint of New Design
Originals Corporation and distributed exclusively in North America by Fox Chapel
Publishing Company, Inc., 800-457-9112, 903 Square Street, Mount Joy, PA 17552,
and in the United Kingdom by Grantham Book Service, Trent Road, Grantham,
Lincolnshire, NG31 7XQ.

INTRODUCTION

Having written our first book, *Decorative Paint Finishes*, which dealt exclusively with interior surfaces, the task of writing a book on exterior decorating seemed daunting! Our initial thoughts were that the only variation you can have on the outside of your house is a change of color every few years when the ever-necessary maintenance is required. However, this simple need to maintain the exterior of one's property sparked some exciting ideas that grew and became more interesting as we looked at the possibilities.

At some stage every year all home owners have to repair the damage caused by harsh weather, be it cold or heat. We haul out the necessary equipment and go off to the local hardware store to buy the appropriate paint and other items to do the job. Fortunately, advanced technology has produced paints that are capable of providing far more than just a change of color. We found new, improved products that can be manipulated to create remarkable decorative finishes, yet still withstand the forces of nature to the same extent as traditional exterior paints.

In *Outdoor Paint Techniques & Faux Finishes* we have explored the possibilities of decorating outside the home, and introduce a variety of projects that are fun, cheap, versatile, simple and effective. This book will take you through the decoration of your outdoor living areas, and give you new ideas on the use of colors, textures and effects. We also show how you can enhance your patio or garden walls, pots, planters and fountains with a variety of paint effects.

Marina Niven & Louise Hennigs

COLOR

Wherever we travel in the world, we notice how the colors used to decorate buildings and homes can define a nationality and create a sense of place. Color is also a reflection of climate. Bright strong colors are used in hot, sun-drenched countries, while in cooler, duller climates the color palette is more subdued.

Putting Color into Context

When looking at historic cultures and traditions around the world, we notice distinct differences in how people decorated their homes and dwellings, and may wonder why such distinctions existed. There are too many reasons to detail here, but the most obvious ones are climate, cultural variations, and the availability of raw materials, including colors. Traditionally, paint was made using pigments available from the earth and from plants, so color choices were determined by the natural environment.

Historic Uses of Color

Natural pigments, which were used throughout the ancient world, are basically earth colors in shades of brown, red oxide, yellow ochre, and black. As exploration and trade opened up new, often exotic lands, different color pigments were discovered. The pigments from each geographic area varied slightly, so specific names were used to differentiate them. Many of these names—such as Venetian red, burnt sienna, and Oxford ochre—are still used today. The advent of technology and the use of synthetic pigments mean that any conceivable color can now be manufactured.

In recent years, a heightened sense of awareness has led to the restoration and preservation of many beautiful old buildings. This, in turn, has prompted conservationists and historians to study traditional uses of color around the world. With the aid of historic records and actual samples taken from the walls and ceilings of buildings, many of the older painting traditions have been revived.

Crisp white trim sets off soft pastel façades.

When contemplating exterior decorating effects, look at your natural surroundings: plants, flowers, fruits, and vegetables can all be used as inspiration when it comes to choosing colors that are in harmony with the world around you.

Some international paint companies have added "traditional" colors to their ranges, making it possible to recreate the authentic decoration of a region. These paint ranges vary from one country to the next, but their names associate them with a particular cultural legacy, such as "Heritage" and the "National Trust" in the UK, and "Williamsburg" in the USA.

Think of the soft grays and blues of Scandinavia, the dusty pinks and ochres of Italy, the stark whitewashed walls and blue trims of Greece, the red barns of Pennsylvania, USA and the vibrant colors of Mexico—each of these presents vivid visual images that are commonly associated with that particular location.

It makes sense to take inspiration from your immediate surroundings, not only architecturally and culturally, but also geographically and from the natural environment. Consider the style of your home, look at the plants in your garden, and at nearby fields, forests, or mountains before deciding on a color scheme.

The Color Wheel

Specific terms are used to describe color. The word *hue* is used to distinguish one color from another; red and green, for example, are different hues. *Primary colors*—red, blue, and yellow—are hues. These three colors are called primary because they cannot be created by mixing other colors.

They can, however, be mixed to create *secondary colors*—purple, green, and orange. These six colors are the basic colors, or hues, of a standard color wheel.

Each primary color lies opposite a secondary color on the color wheel (i.e. red opposite green, yellow opposite purple, blue opposite orange). These are called *complementary colors*, because when they are placed next to each other and mixed optically they complement each other by standing out and appearing brighter. For example, a decorator may introduce green accents to provide the complementary color in a predominantly pink area.

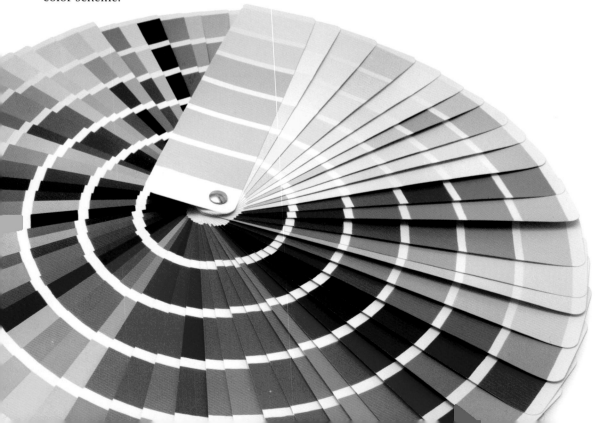

When complementary colors are mixed together as paint, however, they become muddy gray, effectively neutralizing each other.

A *tertiary color* is a mixture of a primary and a secondary color. For example, purple mixed with red will create a reddish purple, or blue mixed with green will create a bluish green. Tertiary colors have altered in hue but are still pure in their depth and color.

Tints, Tones, Values, and Shades
By adding black or white to any color on the color wheel, a new range of exciting colors emerges.

When white is added to a color or hue, it becomes paler and lighter and is called a *tint*. For example, white added to red creates pink. Depending on how much white is added, the pink will have a pale or deep tonal value.

Tone is a term that is frequently used in the same context as value, to refer to the depth or intensity of a particular color.

When black is added to a color it becomes darker and is called a *shade*. The color will vary in value depending on how much black is added.

Colors are categorized into *warm* and *cool*. Warm usually refers to reds, oranges, yellows, and colors that contain them. Cool colors can overlap, making it possible to have warm yellow-greens or cool purple-reds.

Earthy Tones
Earthy colors are derived from natural pigments found in the earth. Yellow ochre, raw and burnt sienna, raw and burnt umber, Indian red, Venetian red, and chrome oxide green are found in clay or stone. When ground to a fine powder, they can be mixed with a binder to make paint.

Natural earth tones are inspired by, and in harmony with, the environment.

The first artists, who made their marks in the form of rock paintings, used natural pigments mixed with animal fat, blood, milk, or plant sap to create a usable mixture. Chalk was used for white and carbon for black.

Color Mixing

It is important to experiment with mixing paint if you want to create your own unique colors.

Don't be alarmed if you find that your mixture does not produce the color you thought it would. In theory, two primary colors can be mixed to create a secondary color. In practice, however, the result can often be duller than expected.

With the development of synthetic pigments, virtually any variation of a hue or shade is commercially available. A full range of colors in artists' oils, acrylics, gouache, and watercolors can be bought at art stores. The following basic colors will provide the fullest mixing range:

REDS

Cadmium red
Vermilion
Alizarin crimson
Venetian red
Indian red
Burnt sienna

YELLOWS

Cadmium yellow
Lemon yellow
Yellow ochre
Raw sienna

BLUES

Cobalt blue
Cerulean blue
Prussian blue
French ultramarine

GREENS
Terre verte
Chromium oxide green
Phthalocyanine green

BROWNS
Raw umber
Burnt umber

TITANIUM WHITE

LAMP BLACK

Complementary colors blend without becoming muddy.

Black mixed with yellow produces
an olive green shade.

When acrylic paint is diluted with
water, a wash is created.

Hardware and paint supply stores have many of
these colors available in the form of universal
tints, which can be used to create colors in
water- or oil-based interior or exterior paints.

When mixing colors, it is very important to
establish which type of paint you are going to
use—oil- or water-based. Remember to use the
appropriate pigments to change colors and the
correct solvent to dilute the paint and clean
the tools.

Tips on Mixing Paints

- When mixing a pale color or tint, start
  with a white base and add small quantities
  of the color. Depending on their pigment
  composition, some colors are stronger than
  others. If you start with the color and add
  white to it, you could end up using a lot of
  white paint to get it pale enough.

- Black is not always the best option to darken
  other colors, as it can often change them
  completely or make them dull. For example,
  adding black to yellow turns it olive green.
  Rather use raw or burnt umber, or even a
  darker hue in the same family. Yellow ochre or
  burnt sienna will produce a darker shade that
  is rich and lively.

- If a color is too bright or crisp in its natural
  state—for example, bright green—add a few
  drops of its complementary color (in this case
  red), to obtain a slight dulling without making
  the color muddy. Complementary colors can
  also be used to cool a warm color, or add
  warmth to a cool color.

- Pastel colors premixed by a paint supplier tend
  to be very "sweet" and ice cream-like. Adding
  a drop or two of either raw umber or the
  complementary color (for example, a drop of
  orange into blue) will reduce the glare without
  changing the overall effect of the color.

The following rules apply to both water- and
oil-based paints:

- Use a brilliant white base when mixing
  pale colors.

- Use a transparent base when mixing
  dark colors.

Using Universal Tints to Color Paint

Universal tints, which are very easy to use, are the only colorants that can be used in both oil- and water-based paints.

1. Add a few drops of the appropriate universal tints to a container filled with either oil- or water-based paint. Remember, if a pale color is required, start with a white base, if a dark color is required, start with a transparent base.

2. Stir the paint well. Paint a test patch on a piece of card and dry it with a hair dryer. (Oil-based paint will take longer to dry than water-based paint.) At this point you will notice that the dry color is different from the wet color. The degree of difference will depend on the type of paint used and the surface onto which it is applied.

3. Adjust the paint mixture by adding small quantities of universal tint, blending each addition well, until you achieve the desired color.

Using Artists' Oils to Color Paint

Artists' oils can only be used to color oil-based paint, glaze or varnish. They give a much purer color than universal tints and are the best paints to use for intricate decorative finishes such as tortoiseshell, lapis lazuli, and malachite.

1. Squeeze about 1¼" (30mm) of a single color, or a combination of colors, onto a palette. Using a palette knife, mix them together until the desired color is achieved.

2. Scrape the color mixture into a small bowl or jar and add enough mineral spirits to dilute it to the consistency of thin cream, removing all the lumps.

3. Keep adding a few drops of the color mixture to the base paint (white alkyd or transparent glaze) until the desired color is achieved.

A few drops of a drier can be added to the paint to speed up the drying process.

Mixing white with a pure color creates a paler color.

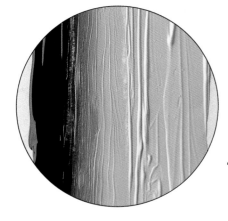

Raw umber takes the "sweetness" out of a pale or pastel color.

Universal tint mixed with water-based emulsion.

Using Artists' Acrylic to Color Paint

Artists' acrylic is water-based and can only be used to color water-based paint, glaze, or varnish.

Some acrylic colors are more opaque than others and can produce a cloudy effect when used to stain transparent glaze or varnish.

1. Squeeze about 1¼" (30mm) of a single color, or a combination of colors, onto a palette. Using a palette knife, mix them together until the desired color is achieved.

2. Scrape the color mixture into a small bowl or jar and add enough water to dilute it, mixing it well to remove all the lumps.

3. Keep adding a few drops of the mixture to the base paint (white paint, transparent glaze, or varnish) until the desired color is achieved.

Different colors liven up a wall.

Commercially Mixed Colors

If you decide not to mix your own colors, you can make use of the vast spectrum of commercially produced colors that are readily available from your local paint supplier.

Most paint manufacturers mix paints to order and have coded paint swatches, which are available in a fan deck or as individual swatches. Use the swatches to match fabrics or existing colors. When you have reached a decision, a paint supplier will mix up any colors you need, in the type of paint most suitable for the particular project you have in mind.

It is advisable to start off with the smallest amount of paint that the store is prepared to mix—usually one quart or liter. Paint a test patch onto sample board or directly onto the wall. A sample board can be made from a smooth piece of hardboard or Masonite that has been primed and undercoated with the same products used on the walls. Very often, the test color will dry differently from the printed swatch, depending on the type of paint or the wall's surface.

Blue pigment mixed with whitewash is traditional in India.

By making a sample board you can check whether the color will work in different lighting—during the day, with artificial light, at night, or in shadow. You can also use the sample board to test decorative techniques. Once you are satisfied with the color and the technique, buy the amount of paint required to complete the project.

MATERIALS AND EQUIPMENT

Glazes, paints, varnishes, and brushes are among the materials and equipment needed for the decorative paint finishes described in this book. Most of the items can be found at your local paint dealer or art store, although some of the finishing brushes and tools may have to be sourced from specialty decorative supply stores.

Paint

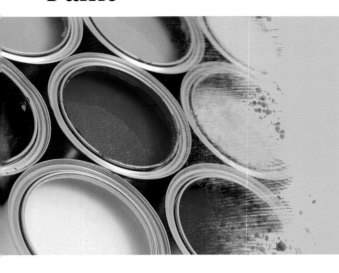

When choosing equipment and materials, use the best products you can afford. The better the tools, the easier it will be to master the techniques. Paint manufacturers produce so many different types of paint that choosing the right one for a particular task can be daunting when confronted with the varieties available. It therefore helps to have a basic understanding of paint, its composition, uses, and applications, before beginning a project.

All paints are made up of a pigment which provides color, a binder or medium in which the pigment is suspended and which binds the paint to the surface, and a solvent which dilutes the mixture to make it flow smoothly and evenly. The solvent evaporates in the drying process and leaves an even, dry coating on the surface. The durability, hardness, and absorbency of the painted surface depends on the type of pigment, binder, and solvent used.

Water-Based Emulsion

In the past, houses were painted both inside and outside with a paint called whitewash or distemper.

Water-based emulsion is a popular and widely available house paint.

This was a simple mixture of lime or chalk, hide glue (also called size), and water. Alternatively, limestone was soaked in water, which naturally heated to a boiling mass, and animal fat was added as a binder. The mixture was allowed to subside and ferment until it was ready for use. Natural pigments, like ochre or red oxide, could be added to give it color. These natural ingredients have now been replaced by synthetic substitutes which make paints more durable and easier to use.

Paint is available in many different finishes, ranging from flat/matte to midsheen/eggshell/satin. Some paint manufacturers also produce high-gloss water-based paints. All water-based paints can be diluted with water and any equipment used can be cleaned with water. Once a water-based paint has dried, it is no longer water soluble.

Water-based paint

ALTERNATIVE NAMES

Paint	latex, emulsion, vinyl emulsion, polyvinylacrylic (PVA)
Pigment	synthetic or natural powder color
Binder	acrylic resin
Solvent	water

When preparing to mix paints, make sure that you have enough suitable containers, plates, or small dishes in which to mix the paints, solvents, and glazes. It is also useful to keep a supply of latex surgical gloves available to use when you are doing messy techniques.

Artists' Acrylic Paint ▼
This is a water-soluble paint that comes in tubes and can be used either on its own, for painting small-scale items such as furniture, or as a colorant in water-based paint. Artists' acrylic can also be diluted with water and used as a color wash.

Water-Mixable Oil Color ▼
This is a new product consisting of oil paint that thins with water and cleans with soap and water. The drying time is much longer than artists' acrylic.

Artists' acrylic paint.

Water-mixable oil color.

Water-Based Glaze ▶

Water-based glaze (also called acrylic scumble glaze) is a recent addition to the list of decorative paint materials. It is sometimes used as a substitute for oil glaze. Often called acrylic medium, this transparent gel-like substance appears milky when wet, but dries to a clear finish. It can be colored and is diluted with water. Water-based glaze retards the drying process of waterbased paints, allowing more time to create decorative finishes.

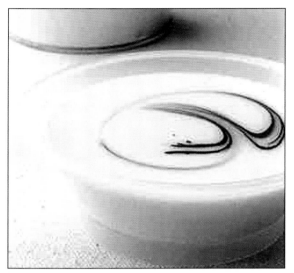
Water-based glaze.

Water-Based Varnish ▶

Water-based varnish is a very useful medium, as it is quick drying and durable. It protects all water-based paint finishes and is available in a flat/matte or mid sheen/suede finish.

It is a milky color when wet, but dries completely clear when applied over the surface in a thin, even layer. If water-based varnish is applied too thickly, it will appear cloudy when dry. This varnish does not discolor with age, which has made it more popular than oil-based varnishes.

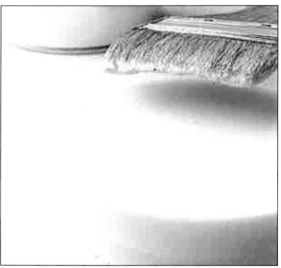
Water-based varnish.

Oil-Based Paint

Oil-based paint is durable and used for interior walls in high-traffic areas, as well as for protecting interior and exterior woodwork. In the past, there was only one type of oil paint, but it is now available in flat/matte, mid sheen/semi-gloss/satin/suede/eggshell, and gloss variations.

Some manufacturers have produced a variety of sheens with modifications for easier application and quicker drying time, or non-drip, nonstir thixotropic (gel-based) paint. It is always advisable to ask your paint supplier to recommend the correct type of paint for a specific purpose.

Artists' Oil Paints ▼

These are primarily used for painting on canvas, but are an excellent source of pure color for tinting oil-based paints and glazes. They are also available in a students' quality at a cheaper price, but the colors are not as saturated or as strong as the artists' quality. Artists' oils can be extended with linseed oil and diluted with mineral spirits.

Oil-based paint

ALTERNATIVE NAMES

Paint alkyd, enamel

Pigment synthetic or natural powder color

Binder synthetic resin or drying oil

Solvent mineral spirits

Paint manufacturers produce a contractors' quality and a more superior quality paint. The difference is often noticeable in the product's durability and price (contractors' quality is cheaper). Some cheaper water-based paints are dry, dull, and chalky and often too absorbent for decorative paint finishes. However, others dry as strong as any oil-based paint and can be used as a base for oil-based decorative techniques.

Artists' oil paint.

Oil-based varnish.

Oil-Based Varnish ▲

Oil-based varnish is used to form a protective coating on painted surfaces and woodwork. Polyurethane varnish is the most commonly used all-purpose oil-based varnish, and is available in flat/matte, semi-sheen/suede, or gloss. Oil-based varnish is yellow and darkens with age, which must be taken into consideration when it is used to protect a colored surface. (For example, a pale blue decorative finish could discolor to green with age.) It can, however, be colored with artists' oils. There are many types of oil-based varnish (such as yacht varnish which is very dark and weather resistant), as well as a variety of wood-stain varnishes.

Oil-Based Glaze ▶

Often referred to as scumble glaze, this is a transparent medium used over a base coat of oil-based paint to create decorative finishes. It can be colored with diluted artists' oils or universal tints. Before it is mixed to the required strength, scumble glaze is a creamy color and thick. It dries quite transparent, allowing the base coat to show through, which makes it suitable for a variety of decorative finishes, such as faux marbling. When it is mixed according to formula it flows easily and can hold a pattern or mark without dripping. Scumble glaze cannot be used on its own as a paint or varnish as it has no inherent properties. It must always be mixed with oil-based paint (artists' oils for transparent color; alkyd for opaque color) and mineral spirits in equal parts (1:1:1).

Storing Paint

When you have finished painting, make sure both the container's rim and the edge of the lid are free of paint. Press the lid down and give it a few knocks with a hammer to secure it. This will keep air out and stop a skin from forming on the paint's surface.

Store paint, glaze, and varnish away from direct heat or sunlight. Make sure all containers are labeled with their contents and where they were used, so that you can find them easily.

If a skin forms on the surface of old paint, remove it and strain the remaining paint through a stocking to remove any lumps.

Oil-based glaze.

Other Materials

POWDER PIGMENTS
Ground-up pigments give a very pure color and are often used to make paint. Earth-colored pigments are sometimes used in antiquing.

WHITING (CALCIUM CARBONATE)
This is a white pigment used to color both water- and oil-based paints. Transparent bases do not contain whiting. It is also used to stop *cissing* (the spattering effect which occurs when a water-based finish is applied to an oil-based surface).

Thixotropic oil-based paint.

ROTTENSTONE
Rottenstone is a fine, light brown powder which is used as a mild abrasive to give texture to some antiquing techniques. Pale gray tile grout powder is a good substitute if rottenstone is not available.

SHELLAC
Shellac is a varnish made from the sticky resin of the lac beetle. It is normally dark brown in color, but is also available in a range of orange colors, or bleached clear. In its dry state it comes in flake form, or as little beads called seedlac. It dissolves in denatured alcohol to become a soft varnish. It is also used to seal knots in raw wood. Knotting is a good commercial substitute for shellac.

DENATURED ALCOHOL/METHYLATED SPIRITS
This is ethyl alcohol with methyl violet added to it to make it poisonous and undrinkable. It is used to dissolve shellac and clean off dried emulsion paint. It is also used in some solvent-release techniques.

Rottenstone, shellac, and powder pigments are used for special finishes.

Brushes and Special Equipment

Brushes are manufactured in a range of sizes, shapes, and qualities and have various uses. The most commonly found brushes are those used for household painting and varnishing. Artists' brushes are more purpose-specific and used for oil, acrylic, or watercolor painting. Specialty brushes for decorative paint finishes can be obtained from local paint dealers or art stores.

All brushes are similarly constructed, although the shape, size, and type of bristle may vary. The filament, or bristle, is fixed into the ferrule (the metal piece holding the filament) with epoxy resin. The handle is attached with rivets or nails. Where the filaments enter the ferrule, fillers separate them, allowing the brush to hold more paint. Brushes are made with natural filaments, such as animal hair or bristle, or synthetic filaments of nylon or polyester. Natural filaments are more durable and give a better paint finish, but are more expensive than brushes with synthetic filaments.

Brush Care

The brushes required for the finishes described in this book are costly, so it pays to treat them well and clean them thoroughly each time they are used.

If your budget allows, buy two sets of decorators' brushes—one set for white paint only and the other for use with colored paints.

Some brushes are specifically made for water-based paints and others for oil-based paints. Try to keep these separate because "water-based" brushes are often made with nylon filaments and will last longer if they are only washed in water.

The first step in brush care is learning to use the brush correctly.

- When loading the paintbrush (i.e. dipping it into the paint), do not submerge the filaments more than halfway. If paint gets into the filaments where they are attached to the ferrule, the brush will be difficult to clean and its life span will be shortened.

- Never stir paint with a brush that you are going to use for painting. Always use a stirring stick, a wooden spoon, or a palette knife.

- You may find that paint starts clogging and drying at the top of the filaments, especially if you work on a large area. This cannot be helped, as the paint will automatically work its way up with each brush stroke. That is why it is advisable to have two brushes. When one brush starts clogging with paint, suspend it in the appropriate solvent to clean it, and continue the project using the other brush.

- Most paintbrushes have a hole at the end of the handle. If not, make a hole big enough to take a length of thin wire. When cleaning the brush, suspend the filaments in the solvent, but do not allow the filaments to rest on the bottom of the container as this will cause them to lose their shape.

- If you need a break from painting, either suspend the brush in solvent or wrap it in a piece of plastic to prevent it from drying out. Never leave brushes hanging in mineral spirits as this will cause the filaments to deteriorate.

Washing Brushes

Always wash brushes in the correct solvent for the type of paint used: water-based paint can be washed off with water, and oil-based paint with mineral spirits.

Wash brushes thoroughly at the end of each painting session. When all the paint has been removed, use a mild dishwashing liquid and warm water for the final wash.

Oil-Based Paint

- Prepare two containers of mineral spirits—one for the first wash, to get the bulk of the paint out of the filaments, and the other for a second wash, to ensure that all the paint is removed. After the first wash, squeeze out excess solvent and dry the brush with a rag before washing it again in the clean solvent.

- If there is a stubborn residue of paint near the ferrule, take a wire brush and work it through the filaments, away from the ferrule.

- When all the paint has been washed out in the solvent, wash the brush with mild dishwashing liquid and cold water. Rinse well.

- Get rid of excess water by rolling the brush handle between the palms of your hands.

- Reshape the bristles and hang the brush on a wire hook to dry.

Good brushes need proper care.

Artists' brushes, and round and flat fitches in both nylon and natural bristle, are used for all fine decorative paint finishes.

Water-Based Paint

- Using water as the cleaning solvent, rinse the brush under running water, working the paint out of the filaments with your fingers.

- If there is a stubborn residue of dry paint close to the ferrule, soak the brush in denatured alcohol/methylated spirits and then use a wire brush to work out the dissolved pieces. Denatured alcohol will only dissolve dried water-based paint or any other product that has denatured alcohol as its solvent, such as shellac.

- When all the paint has been removed, wash the brush with mild dishwashing liquid and cold water. Rinse well.

- Get rid of excess water by rolling the brush's handle between the palms of your hands.

- Reshape the bristles and hang the brush on a wire hook to dry.

Caring for Artists' and Specialty Brushes

Never leave brushes standing on their filaments in the cleaning solvent for an extended time, as this will bend the filaments, damage their structure, and make painting difficult. If you are interrupted while painting, rinse the brushes in solvent and wrap them in plastic wrap or a plastic bag to prevent them from drying out. Let them lie flat until they are used again, but not longer than a few hours. If you want specialty brushes to maintain their softness and flexibility, and last a long time, treat them as you would your own hair.

To remove paint, use your fingers to work the appropriate solvent through the filaments, then rinse the brush thoroughly in clean solvent. Wipe off excess solvent on paper towels and then wash with shampoo and conditioner. When the brush is thoroughly clean and rinsed, wipe off excess water and dry with a hair dryer.

Stippling Brush

A stippling brush must be dry when you start working with it. Unlike decorators' brushes, a stippling brush cannot be left in solvent during a break or if it starts clogging with paint because the solvent will be absorbed by the filaments and affect the paint finish. When using a stippling brush, always work with a cloth in your hand and wipe the paint off the filaments after a few dabs. If you need to take a break from painting, it is preferable to wash the brush thoroughly and let it dry completely before using it again.

Flogging and Dragging Brushes

These brushes can withstand more paint than stippling or softening brushes. However, the paint build-up during flogging or dragging must be checked, as it will alter the character of the finish. Keep a dry cloth nearby to wipe off excess paint.

Softening Brushes
(Japanese Hake or Dusting Brush)
These specialty brushes should never be allowed to gather paint. Only the tips of the filaments should skim the surface of the glaze, softening the glazed surface but without picking up any paint. If excess paint collects on them, it must be washed off so that the quality of the brush is maintained.

Storing Brushes

Some brushes come with a protective cardboard sleeve and once they are dry, it is advisable to keep them in this sleeve, or wrapped in paper, as this will help to maintain the shape of the filaments, thereby prolonging the life of the brush.

Specialty Brushes

When dry, wrap the brushes in tissue paper or cloth, taking care not to crush the filaments.

Artists' Brushes

Take a drop of liquid soap between your thumb and forefinger and coat the filaments with a thin layer of soap, making sure they come together in a neat point; the soap will dry and protect them. Stand the brushes, filaments up, in a jar or keep them in a pouch. Remember to wash the soap off before using a brush again.

Brushes for Decorative Finishes

Standard decorators' brushes (2, 5 & 9) Used for large and small areas.

Standard flat decorators' brushes (6) Use a 4" to 5" (100 to 125mm) flat brush for painting walls or large areas.

Sash brushes (8) For painting narrow surfaces and woodwork with oil- or water-based paints. They can also be used for varnishing.

Specialty oval or flat varnish brushes (1, 3 & 4) Designed to hold a lot of varnish.

Artists' fitches (see photograph on page 29) Can be flat, round, or filbert (pointed), natural or synthetic, and are used for all fine decorative work in oil or acrylic.

Badger softener (15) Used to soften and blend marks in oil-and water-based glazes.

Japanese hake (16 & 17) Used for softening and blending colors.

Flogger (10) Creates a broken texture, resembling wood, when flicked against wet glaze. Horsehair filaments make it very flexible. (Can also be used for dragging.)

Dragger (18) Filaments are bunched in the ferrule; natural filaments on one side, nylon filaments on the other.

Dusting brush (14) Usually made from hog hair, it can be used for small areas of stippling and softening.

Stippling brush (12) Available in various sizes and used for dispersing glaze evenly over a surface and eliminating brush strokes.

Stencil brush (13) A short-haired brush with stiff, tightly packed bristles, designed to hold small amounts of paint which is applied through a stencil with a brisk stabbing action.

Cutting brush (not shown) The filaments are cut at an angle for reaching into edges and corners.

A selection of decorators' brushes, sash brushes, and varnish brushes.

Specialty brushes include stipplers, floggers, hakes, badgers, stencil, and dusting brushes.

DECORATIVE FINISHES

Decorative paint techniques used outdoors have to withstand harsh weather conditions, so their lifespan is shorter than interior finishes. With this in mind, have fun with different techniques. Experiment on smaller items before making major changes, and remember to select the appropriate finish for the area or object to be painted.

DECORATIVE FINISHES

PLASTER

Decorative finishes on exterior walls usually involve painting the outside of the house, or patio and garden walls. Most of the techniques described in this section are suitable for walls built from bricks and finished with cement plaster, but many can be applied on other surfaces, provided these are well prepared.

FINISHES

Surface Preparation

The first step in preparing your walls for a new finish is to establish what condition they are already in. If you are not sure what type of paint has been previously used, a simple test of whether a wall has been painted with an oil- or water-based paint is to take a rag or cotton ball soaked in denatured alcohol and rub a small spot on the wall in an inconspicuous place. If the existing paint is water-based, it will rub off onto the cloth.

Pre-Painted Walls in Good Condition

Walls that are in good condition require minimum preparation. Make sure they are clean and dust free, as exterior walls can have a greasy film caused by general pollution, such as exhaust fumes. Wash the walls with a solution of TSP (trisodium phosphate) and warm water, rinse with clean water and allow to dry. A good wall will not need to be primed (prepared or made ready).

If you are using the same paint as used before, you can paint directly onto the wall. However, although a wall that has been previously painted in water-based paint can support either water-based or oil-based paint, the reverse does not apply.

Pre-Painted Walls in Poor Condition

If the walls are in poor condition, with peeling paint and large cracks, careful preparation is required.

Scrape off loose paint, ensuring that the plaster does not pull off. To fill a crack, first enlarge it by inserting the point of a triangular scraper and then draw it along the crack. Dust it out and fill with an all-purpose or ready mixed filler (spackle). If the crack is large, fill it in stages

Ochre walls glow in the warmth of the sun.

Plaster walls must be in good condition before painting starts.

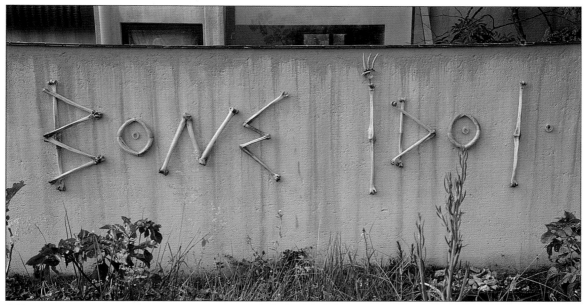

A blue color wash and some creative graffiti have turned a previously plain wall into an eye-catching feature. Using the right paints on a well-prepared surface is the basis for all decorative paint effects.

because the compound shrinks as it dries. When the filler is dry, sand it smooth and spot-prime the patched area.

Walls Pre-Painted with Oil-Based Paint

For walls painted with an oil-based paint, use sandpaper on a sanding block to rub down the wall. This roughens the surface, creating a "key" or "tooth," essential so that the new layers of paint can bond with the old. After sanding, wash the walls with a solution of TSP and warm water to remove all traces of dust. The walls are now ready for two coats of base color in the appropriate type of paint.

New Walls

It is extremely important to allow newly plastered walls to dry out completely before beginning to paint, as this allows the salts and chemicals to work their way to the surface.

Newly plastered walls do not have to be washed, only lightly dusted. Limewash can be applied directly to the raw wall, but if you use water- or oil-based paint, the wall should first be primed with a coat of plaster primer or sealer (ask your paint dealer to recommend

an appropriate product, as these differ among manufacturers). When the primer has dried, apply a coat of universal undercoat.

Walls Previously Painted with Limewash

If you already have limewashed walls, continue to use this finish if possible. Limewash should only be applied to walls made from porous brick, or plaster. Limewash allows walls to breathe and deal with dampness naturally through the seasons.

If you are going to paint a limewashed wall with a modern acrylic, water-based, or oil-based paint, make sure there is no dampness in the wall. As soon as you change to a modern household paint you seal the wall with a plastic coat and it can no longer breathe. If there is any moisture trapped in the wall, it will eventually cause the paint to blister and peel off.

To prepare a new wall for limewash, brush it down with a stiff brush to remove any dust or loose dirt. Once free of dust, the surface will need a coat of bonding liquid. Then follow the instructions starting on the next page for preparing a new wall.

Limewash

MATERIALS
- Lime putty or powder (see Tip #1)
- Natural pigment in your chosen color (see Tip #2)
- Water

EQUIPMENT
- 2 large buckets
- Small container with a lid
- Block brush
- Strainer or stocking
- Power drill with a mixing attachment, or a kitchen whisk
- Protective latex gloves
- Protective clothing
- Safety goggles
- Plastic drop sheets or cloth dust sheets to protect surfaces

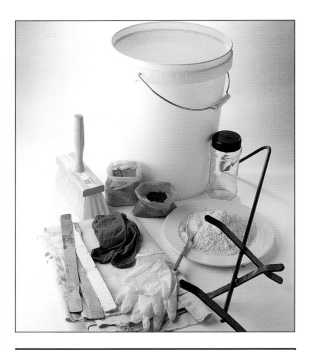

For centuries, limewash was used as the preferred exterior covering of houses all over the world. Made of lime (a common building material) and water, it was readily available, cheap, and easy to use. Thus it was not a problem to limewash homes every year—a practice still common in parts of Greece. The regular application of lime strengthens walls, allowing them to breathe and damp to escape.

Lime produces lovely subtle shades of color when tinted with natural earth pigments and dries to a soft, matte, slightly translucent finish that is characteristic of limewash. It also ages well and the color will fade back into the surface with time, unlike modern synthetic paints that eventually peel and flake off.

With the advent of modern paint technology, limewash lost its popularity and was pushed aside as an old-fashioned material, but in recent years there has been a trend toward reviving older painting methods that use natural, environmentally friendly products as opposed to synthetic, toxic materials. Paint companies around the world are now producing natural products in an easy-to-use format that is ideal for DIY enthusiasts.

Tip #1 *Lime in its burned state (called quicklime—another name for calcium oxide) needs to be slaked (soaked in water) before it can be diluted to limewash. The slaking process is dangerous and best left to the professionals, as lime boils vigorously when it is added to water, reaching very high temperatures. These days, most hardware stores sell slaked lime in powder or putty form.*

Tip #2 *Yellow ochre dries to a soft butter color, red oxide gives a soft pink, and a mixture of the two creates a subtle terra-cotta. Experiment with whatever earth pigments are readily available. Check whether your paint dealer stocks any synthetic pigments that are compatible with lime.*

Tip #3 *Wet lime is as caustic as household bleach, so always wear protective clothing when using lime and avoid splashing it into your eyes.*

TECHNIQUE

1 In the first bucket, mix together the lime putty or powder and water. Use a drill with a mixing attachment to work out all the lumps until the mixture has the consistency of milk. Be sure to wear protective clothing as the drill will cause much splashing.

2 The pigment powder must be diluted in water before it can be added to the lime. Place a few tablespoons of pigment in a cup of water and shake it up in a small container (a glass jar with a screw top lid is ideal).

3 Stretch the stocking over the top of the clean bucket and pour the lime mixture through it to strain any lumps that might not have dissolved. Then add the pigment.

4 With a clean block brush, sprinkle water over the area of the wall that is to be painted. This will reduce the absorbency and give you more time to work with the paint.

Tip #4 *Limewash is very dark when it is wet but dries out drastically to a pale shade. Test your color on a sample board and dry it with a hair dryer.*

5 Use the block brush to apply the limewash over the surface as evenly as possible, working in vertical strips from top to bottom, trying not to stop halfway. The painting must be done in small areas at a time as the plaster surface is thirsty and dries quickly. Stir the paint frequently.

6 When the first coat has dried, re-dampen the surface and apply the second coat in the same way as the first.

Tip #5 *Do not overwork each coat, as this disturbs the previous layers. Do not try to reduce the number of coats by making the limewash thicker, as it will only crack and fall off. The principle is that each thin layer soaks into the previous one, becoming one with the original plaster wall, and thereby strengthening the whole structure.*

NOTE: *No sealer is required for limewashing. Rain affects the drying process, so choose a fine day to paint, but avoid direct sunlight, as this will cause the surface to dry too quickly.*

The soft shades of pink on this island home can easily be achieved with a limewash finish.

Layered Color Washing

MATERIALS
- White water-based emulsion
- Acrylic scumble glaze
- Universal tints
- Water

EQUIPMENT
- 3 containers for mixing colors
- 4" (100mm) decorators' paintbrush
- Paint tray
- Plastic bags to cover paint tray
- Chamois
- Protective latex gloves
- Plastic or cloth drop cloths to protect surfaces

Color washing is one of the oldest and most frequently used decorative paint finishes, but strictly speaking, this is a technique best-suited to interiors. The reason for this is that it requires paint to be diluted with water. This process weakens the composition of the paint and thus its resistance to the elements. However, in our experience of applying this finish to exterior walls, the only thing we noticed was a slight fading of the color, and that was over a 10-year period. Adding modern water-based scumble glaze to water-based emulsion eliminates the necessity of having to dilute the paint excessively with water, because the scumble glaze maintains most of its original durability. The effect is similar to limewashing.

As most modern houses are painted with synthetic paints and cannot be limewashed in the traditional manner, color washing is a good alternative. If enough layers of glaze are applied and the correct colors are used, it is possible to achieve the soft, translucent, slightly mottled effect of old limewash.

TECHNIQUE

1 Using three containers, make the glazes by mixing equal quantities of white water-based emulsion and acrylic scumble glaze. Add universal tints to two of the mixtures. (Select colors from the same section of the color spectrum, as opposite colors will give a dull appearance. See page 12.) Make the third mixture a very diluted pale milky color for the final coat. Add enough water to each of the glazes to obtain the consistency of cream.

2 Starting with any one of the colors, use a crosshatch motion to apply the glaze to an area no bigger than 4 sq. ft. (60cm²) at a time. Work at random, allowing the brush strokes to remain visible.

3 Before the first coat is dry, apply the second color in randomly placed honeycomb patches, allowing the first color to show through. Blend and soften the edges between the two colors. Allow both coats to dry thoroughly. You can apply as many, or as few, colors as you like but the last coat of glaze (described in step 4) is very important to achieve a good finish.

4 Using the pale glaze, paint the entire wall with an even stroke to knock back the colors and soften the effect so that you do not see any brush strokes, and the wall has the powdery translucent appearance of limewash. If the glaze drips, dab the surface lightly with a chamois.

The soft translucent effect of color washing turns a tap into a feature.

Antiquing and Distressing

MATERIALS
- White water-based emulsion paint
- Universal tints: in raw umber, burnt sienna, raw sienna, yellow ochre, black, or premixed color emulsion
- Acrylic scumble glaze
- Water

EQUIPMENT
- 3 containers to mix colors
- 6" and 4" (150 and 100mm) paintbrushes
- Extra paintbrushes
- Clean newsprint and brown paper
- Coarse-grade (80 grit) sandpaper
- Protective latex gloves
- Plastic or cloth drop cloths to protect surfaces

This section covers a few options to create a beautiful aged and worn effect on plastered and painted walls. With the use of a few simple techniques, the natural weathering process can be simulated in paint.

This look is very popular in country homes and gardens where a feeling of antiquity adds authenticity. These antiquing finishes can be applied to walls that have been base coated in a flat color or to walls finished in the color wash technique shown in the previous section.

Simple Ageing on a Clean Wall

PREPARATION

Paint the wall with a flat base coat of water-based paint in a pale earthy color or off-white.

> **Tip** Test the colors, as water changes the strength of color.

TECHNIQUE

1 Using separate containers, mix equal quantities of water-based emulsion with acrylic scumble glaze and add a few drops of universal tints to obtain the three colors of your choice. These should be darker than the base color, to imitate the dirt and stains that represent "old and worn." Dilute with water to the consistency of cream.

2 With a brush or cloth, wet the section of the wall to be painted. Dip the 4" (100mm) brush into the lightest color and paint a crosshatch pattern in vertical strips about 18" (500mm), allowing the base color to show in places. (Always work outward from corners.)

3 As the paint starts to dry, take the clean, dry 6" (150mm) brush and work the paint into drifts. This creates color build-up that looks like watermarks or stains.

4 Soften the drifts of color by going over the surface lightly with a clean, dry brush. Allow to dry.

5 Using the darker colors and the same method as before, work the paint into areas that would show more ageing, such as corners, or where the walls meet ground or floor.

Exposed Plaster

This technique follows after step 2 described on page 47.

This technique follows after step 2 described on page 47.

TECHNIQUE

1 When the first coat is dry, brush pieces of torn newsprint onto the wall using a clean, damp brush.

2 Paint over the newsprint and the wall with a darker colored paint and then peel off the newsprint to "expose" the base color.

Frottage

This technique creates an uneven painted effect. *Frottage* means "rubbing" in French and involves the application of crumpled brown paper onto a wet painted surface. This is lightly rubbed and then removed, exposing the base color and leaving an impression in the wet paint. Work with a light over-glaze on a dark wall, or vice versa.

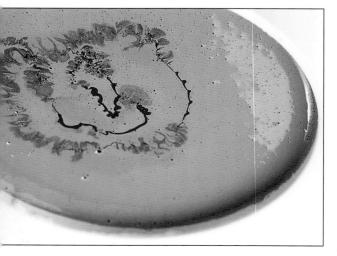

TECHNIQUE

1 Mix a glaze using equal quantities of water-based emulsion and acrylic scumble glaze and dilute it with water to a creamy consistency. Add a few drops of universal tint to obtain the color of your choice. (In this example, a darker glaze has been used over a lighter base coat.) Begin by painting a 3' (1m) strip of wall.

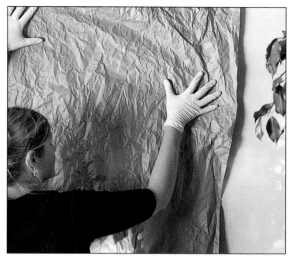

2 Take a length of brown paper, crumple it, smooth it out slightly and then press it onto the wet paint at the top of the wall. Smooth the paper onto the wall using your hands and forearms in a fanning movement, working from the outer edges of the paper toward the center.

3 When you get to the bottom of the wall, peel off the paper from the top down. Continue with the rest of the wall, painting up to the wet edges of the previous panel and using a fresh length of brown paper for each strip. When the walls are completely dry, lightly sand them with coarse sandpaper to remove bumps and irregularities in the plaster and expose some base coat. (Sanding is optional.)

A sunset casts shadows on the walls of this desert home, echoing the red of the sand outside.

Pigmented and Faux Plaster

MATERIALS
- Texturing medium (cement powder pre-tinted to the correct color)
- Optional pigment
- Water

EQUIPMENT
- Block brush
- Mixing paddle
- 5 gal. (20L) bucket
- Protective latex gloves
- Plastic or cloth drop cloths to protect surfaces

Freshly plastered walls, particularly those pigmented with earth colors, have become a popular decorative look. Although it is not a true paint finish, plastering is an effective technique that forms part of some paint effects. Many decorative paint effects attempt to recreate some element of antiquity and the techniques described here emulate old, unpainted, or textured plaster walls.

Applying plaster to large areas is better done by a professional plasterer, but it is fun to experiment in small areas, and working with a trowel can lead to new and interesting finishes. Plaster is available in shades of pink, gray, and white, but by adding powdered pigments to the plaster, darker and more durable colors can be obtained. The pigment, however, must be alkaline-free, otherwise the lime content in the plaster will fade the color in a few months.

Textured plaster adds depth and interest to an otherwise plain wall.

Textured Plaster Using Cement Paint

Textured plaster can be very effective outdoors, as the play of sunlight and shadows caused by the texture can add to the visual depth of color. It also creates an old, country-style look.

Note: This surface is also a good base for antiquing and stone finishes.

TECHNIQUE

1 Using a large bucket, add the pre-tinted cement powder to the water. Follow the manufacturer's instructions for correct proportions. Slowly add the tinted pigment powder, stirring with a mixing paddle to prevent lumps from forming.

2 Wet the area of wall to be painted by brushing over it with a clean, wet block brush. Work on small areas at a time to prevent the plaster from drying out too quickly.

3 Dip the block brush into the cement paint and apply it to the wall, working from top to bottom. If the brush is dragged downward, the texture will be streaky.

4 An alternative method of application is to apply the paint in a crosshatch movement, which will result in a less formal, more rustic texture.

MATERIALS
- Terra-cotta water-based emulsion
- Universal tints: in raw umber, brown, red oxide, yellow
- White water-based emulsion
- Acrylic varnish
- Rottenstone or gray chalk powder
- Water

EQUIPMENT
- 4 containers for mixing colors
- 2" and 1" (50 and 25mm) decorators' paintbrushes
- Sea sponge
- Protective latex gloves
- Plastic or cloth drop cloths to protect surfaces

Terra-cotta

Real terra-cotta planters and decorative urns have become quite costly and, being made of clay, they are fragile. This is a quick and easy way to give inexpensive plastic and cement containers an expensive-looking terra-cotta finish. It is preferable to work on surfaces that have interesting details and moldings as this gives more opportunity for a characteristic finish. (Terra-cotta floor tiles can be painted on a cement floor.)

Preparation

Cement containers must be brushed with a wire brush and primed with universal undercoat. If you do not prime, the painted surface will eventually wear off in places and develop an identity of its own (which, if you are prepared to take the risk, might be attractive). Sand plastic pots with coarse sandpaper to create a key that allows the primer to adhere to the surface. Plastic must be well primed with universal undercoat, as the deterioration of the paint finish on this surface is not attractive.

Tip #1 *Look at real terra-cotta pots, preferably used ones, and note the subtle varying shades of color which give the clay an almost translucent quality. Try to copy these variations when mixing your colors.*

TECHNIQUE

1 Pour the terra-cotta water-based emulsion into three containers. Using a few drops of universal tint, mix up three different tones of terra-cotta. Stir well.

2 Starting with the darkest color, brush the paint onto the entire surface, making sure it gets into all the molded areas. Allow to dry completely.

3 With the lightest color, paint in patches with random brush strokes, allowing the base color to show through. Try not to leave spiky brush marks. Allow to dry.

4 Take the second lightest color and apply with random strokes, as before. As the paint starts to set, continue working the surface with the brush to soften the brush marks. This will knock back the previous shades and create a translucent effect. Allow to dry.

5 Using a clean brush, wet the painted surface with water. This will retard the drying process and make the paint applied in the next step more workable.

6 Pour some white emulsion into a container and dilute with water. Using a small brush and working at a vertical angle from the top, drip the white diluted glaze over sections of the surface, allowing it to run in rivulets and collect in the moldings. This simulates the effect of rain on terra-cotta. Use the clean, dampened sea sponge to mop up excessive dripping.

As the white glaze begins to dry it will fade to the characteristic powdery bloom.

Tip #2 *Add raw umber to acrylic varnish, dilute with water and dribble down to simulate moldy streaks.*

7 Protect the painted surface with a coat of acrylic varnish. Before the varnish is dry, use a dry brush to apply either the rottenstone or chalk powder to the moldings and in drifts around the bottom of the container, to imitate the salty residue that forms on terra-cotta surfaces after a while.

With a bit of paint and creativity, inexpensive cement planters can be turned into elegant terra-cotta pots.

Decorative Patterns on Walls

SHOPPING LIST

MATERIALS
- Emulsion paint: in white or any other color of your choice
- Selection of universal tints
- Water

EQUIPMENT
- 2" and 1" (50 and 25mm) paintbrushes
- Containers for mixing paint
- Tape measure
- Set square
- 1¼" (30mm) masking tape
- Chalk crayon
- Cardboard and marker pen
- Paper and pencil
- Craft knife
- Saw
- Pressed chipboard
- Stencils (optional)
- Nails or screws with masonry anchors
- Waterproof sealer
- Protective latex gloves
- Plastic or cloth drop cloths to protect surfaces

Tip #1 *When painting a border around a door (an architrave), make it run into a block at floor level that is wider than the border, to give a more solid appearance.*

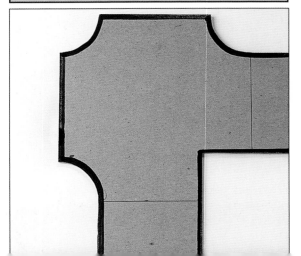

Patterning can be applied to walls in a variety of ways. It can be used to change the overall appearance or simply to accentuate certain features. Patterns can vary from colored lines painted around a window or door, to an intricate stenciled motif running along a wall. Painted patterns can also take the form of a trellis, which can either cover the whole area or can be done in shaped panels to give a plain wall an interesting new dimension.

Painted Borders on Door and Window Surrounds

Using a painted border to accentuate an architectural feature can be very effective. For example, doors and windows can be made to look larger and more important, while different shapes and patterns emphasize the decorative look that one can achieve. Classic examples can be seen in parts of Bavaria and Austria, where the houses are quite simple box-like structures, with rather plain façades and small square or rectangular windows. They are transformed with elaborate window and door surrounds of great beauty. In 18th-century America, stencils were frequently used to enhance decorative borders.

TECHNIQUE

1 Measure a border approximately 5" to 6" (12 to 15cm) wide around the window or door. Using a chalk crayon, draw it directly onto the wall.

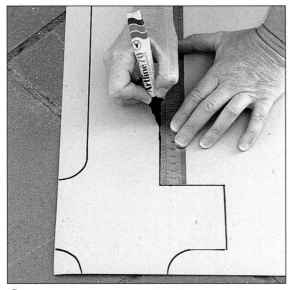

2 Corners can be accentuated with a block or any shape bigger than the border. To make the pattern, first draw the width of the border, then trace the pattern for the corner onto a piece of cardboard and cut a template of your design.

3 Place the template over the right angle at the corner and draw around it. Repeat for all four corners.

Tip #2 *Masking tape can pull paint off walls, so de-tack the tape first by sticking it to a flat fabric surface and then onto the wall. Low-tack tape is also available.*

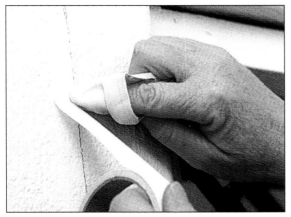

4 Stick masking tape around the outside of the surround you have drawn and rub down the inside edge very well using a piece of cloth wrapped over your finger.

5 Paint the whole border with two coats of water-based emulsion paint, allowing 24 hours drying time between coats.

Pressed Board or Chipboard Window Surrounds

This can be an alternative to painting directly onto the wall.

TECHNIQUE

6 The border can be made to look more three-dimensional by drawing a shadow line underneath and on one side. Mix a small quantity of the border color with a few drops of raw umber universal tint to get the shadow color.

1 Cut four strips of chipboard to the width required for the border around a window or door.

Decorative window treatments.

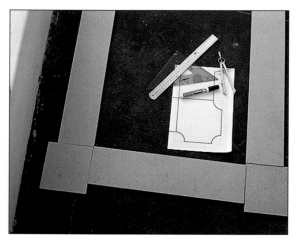

2 Use blocks on the corners to hide the joints. They can be any shape and can be stenciled with a design.

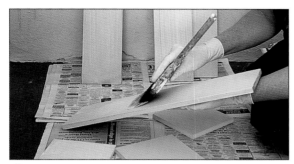

3 Lie the chipboard strips flat and paint them with the necessary undercoat and topcoat.

4 As an option, the whole border or just the corners can be stenciled with decorative patterns.

5 When the boards are dry, position them around the window and attach them to the wall. For wooden houses, the frame can be nailed to the wall; for plaster or brick walls, screws and masonry anchors must be used.

Tip #3 *Wooden board surrounds can also be cut into different shapes and used to decorate the top of a garden wall.*

6 The gaps between the wall and the wood should always be sealed with a waterproof sealer. Touch up the holes left by nails or screws with the appropriate color paint.

With practice, you can move on to quite complex effects, like the wooden motifs that brighten up this door.

MATERIALS

- Paint: 1–3 colors in containers (for best results, use artists' acrylic or water based emulsion)
- Extra background base color to touch up smudges

EQUIPMENT

- Photocopied design
- Stencil card (acetate can also be used)
- Craft knife with sharp pointed blade for cutting stencils
- Cutting mat or thick sheet of glass
- Plastic or foil plates as palettes (one for each color used)
- Brushes: stencil brush; varnish brush; artists' fitch
- Swabs (see Tip #1)
- Pencil and eraser, or chalk
- Ruler or straightedge
- Scissors
- Absorbent paper towel
- Carbon paper
- ¼" (12mm) masking tape
- Low-tack tape, plastic putty, or spray adhesive (glue tack)
- Rags
- Sponge
- Steel wool
- Felt-tip waterproof marker
- Water bucket for washing brushes
- Protective latex gloves
- Plastic or cloth drop cloth to protect surfaces

Tip #1 *To make a swab, take a thin dowel or skewer and attach a square of foam sponge to the end. Cover this with a square of T-shirt fabric and secure it with string or a rubber band, making a lollipop (use one for each color of paint).*

Painted Stencils on a Wall

Stenciling is a very easy and effective way of decorating not only walls, but also floors, furniture, objects, and ornaments. As stencils can be reused, they eliminate having to paint designs by hand. Precut stencils in a variety of designs are readily available from specialty stores and online. Alternatively, designs can be photocopied from pictures, adapted and scaled to the required size. Stencils can be applied to various surfaces with equal success. The surface should be clean with no loose, flaking paint or grease.

Making Your Own Stencil

1 Draw or photocopy a design. Simplify it by outlining areas with a felt-tip marker, so that the sections to be painted can be easily cut out. Decide how many colors you want to use and where they are to be placed. This will determine how many different stencils you have to cut.

2 Paint the flat colors onto the original design and keep it as your master copy.

3 Once you have decided on the design and colors, note the importance of "bridges" at frequent intervals. These are linking pieces that must be evenly spaced between the cut-out windows to hold the design together. If doing a repeat pattern, make several copies of the final design as more than one set of stencils will be required. Transfer the design onto stencil card by using a sharp pencil on carbon paper. Allow a margin of 2" to 4" (5 to 10cm) around the edges of the cut stencil to hold it together.

4 Use a cutting mat or thick piece of glass to press on. Holding a craft knife at a 45° angle for a clean incision, cut out the sections for the first color, starting from the center of the design. Make a separate stencil for each color used.

Tip #2 *An alternative way of making another set of stencils is to use a can of spray paint to spray through the original design onto another piece of stencil card.*

Determining Proportions

If you are making your own stencil and you want the pattern to fit exactly into a given space, you first need to determine the proportions. Measure the wall or area to be painted and divide it into equal sections. You will have to make a rough estimate of how many pattern repeats you will need to fit the area. For example, a 5' (1.5m)–long wall will take approximately six pattern repeats of a 10" (25cm) stencil. (Divide the length of the wall by the size of the stencil to obtain the number of pattern repeats required.) If your stencil is precut, find the center point of the area and, working from this point outward on either side, mark off with chalk the number of repeats that will fit into the space. To disguise any shortfalls in the design, you may have to leave gaps between each stencil, or design a special end or corner piece.

When painting, position the stencil as you did for the measuring process, starting either from the center point and working outward, or from one corner across to the opposite corner.

Tip #3 *A design with many colors needs registration marks on each stencil. Cut registration notches on all the edges of the stencil so that when the individual colors are overlaid, they can be accurately positioned.*

TECHNIQUE

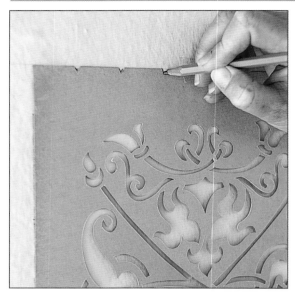

1 Fix the stencil in position with small pieces of low-tack tape. Mark the registration notches with chalk that can be easily wiped off.

2 Have the desired paint ready and decant a small amount of the first color into a foil or plastic plate.

3 Dip the stencil brush into the paint and dab on a double layer of absorbent paper towel or newspaper. The brush should be half dry. Use a light circular movement to rub paint through the cutout sections of the stencil onto the wall. Work from the edges toward the center.

4 A swab (or lollipop) is another effective way of stenciling instead of using a brush. Dip the swab into paint and roll out on the foil plate or paper to remove excess paint. Do not start stenciling with too much paint as it will seep under the stencil and smudge. Use the swab on its side and dab it across the stencil.

5 Always clean the stencil before you reposition it and when you have finished. Use a damp cloth to wipe inward toward the windows. In this case, the stencil was flipped to repeat the design in the first color. If using a second stencil, have it ready to use while the first one is drying.

6 If any bridges have broken, lay the stencil on a flat surface then place a piece of masking tape over the break. Turn it over and repeat on the reverse side. Press the tape down firmly and recut the bridge.

Final Touches

If paint has smudged or seeped under the bridges and edges of the stencil, touch up with an artists' brush and the base color. Dilute the darkest color or raw umber and wash over the surface with a sponge to soften the design.

When the paint is dry, steel wool can be rubbed lightly over the pattern to age the design, creating a subtle, faded antique finish.

This stencil has aged and faded with time, blending into the wall.

Tip #4 *When stenciling on a rough surface, use paint very sparingly otherwise it will smudge under the bridges. To prevent this, press the stencil down with your finger as you dab with the swab or stencil brush.*

MATERIALS
- Water-based emulsion paint in the background color of the wall or object
- Acrylic scumble glaze for transparency
- Artists' acrylic paints: in raw umber, black
- Universal tints: in raw umber, black, ultramarine
- Optional color paint for the trellis
- Waterproof acrylic varnish

EQUIPMENT
- Containers for mixing paint
- Brushes: decorators' ¾" (15mm) flat bristle brush; artists' ¾" and 1" (15 and 25mm) flat nylon brushes
- Graph paper, plain paper, and tracing paper
- Pencil and eraser
- Water-soluble crayon
- Ruler, straightedge, and measuring tape
- Craft knife
- Masking or low-tack tape
- Rags
- Protective latex gloves
- Plastic or cloth drop cloths to protect surfaces

Trellis
Trellis is an ideal decoration in almost any garden environment. On patio and terrace walls it creates an architectural effect that can transform featureless exterior walls. The range of designs that can be used is virtually limitless and can be adapted to fit any size or shape to enhance plain walls.

The most popular panel design for wooden trellis has a square or diamond shape between the slats, and comes in three different sizes: 2", 4", and 6" (50, 100, and 150mm). Traditional trellis has slats positioned at right angles (90°), but trellis that is elongated into diamond shapes (55° angles) is also very pleasing. Elaborate shapes, such as archways with perspective lines (called illusion panels), can be added. These can be extremely decorative and add another dimension to a wall. Fanlights, rose arches, and columns make an eye-catching focal point on a terrace or patio. Trellis columns placed on either side of, or surrounding, a mural can also be very effective.

TECHNIQUE

1 Measure the wall or object that the trellis will be painted on and draw it to scale on graph paper.

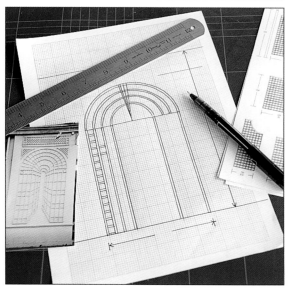

2 Draw or photocopy the design of the trellis and fit it onto the scale drawing of the wall or object. (Catalogs from companies that make and install trellis are full of good designs that can be adapted for your purpose.)

3 Using a ruler, transfer the design to the object or wall. If the object is small, then a simple pencil tracing will suffice. If the trellis is large, it can be scaled up from the photocopy to the right size.

4 Mix the color for the trellis, traditionally a turquoise, green, or white. Then mix two shadowing glazes, one a tone darker than the other. For the darker glaze, add a few drops of raw umber universal tint to acrylic scumble glaze and a little of the trellis color. For the lighter shadow color, add more acrylic scumble glaze.

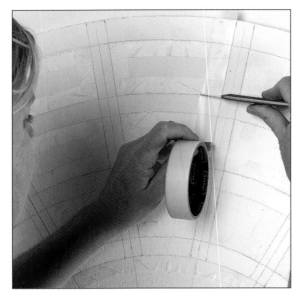

5 Mask off the trellis with low-tack tape. Run the tape down each side of the vertical and horizontal slats and then cut out the cross sections.

6 Paint in the trellis using a flat 1" (25mm) nylon artists' brush. When dry, carefully remove all the tape. When painting white trellis on a white background, mask off the slats horizontally and vertically with ¾" (15mm) low-tack tape. Paint the squares or diamonds between the slats a tone darker than white (add a few drops of raw umber universal tints to white emulsion), then paint in the shadows as described below.

7 Decide which slats are on top, either the vertical or the horizontal, as the shadows change the appearance of the trellis. If the trellis is in squares, the darker shadow will be under the slats and the lighter shadow will be a narrower band on one side. If the trellis is on the diagonal, creating diamonds, then the shadows will only be on one side, opposite the light source.

8 Protect the paintwork with a final coat of waterproof acrylic varnish.

Perspective lines can be used to give an extra dimension to trellis, be it faux or genuine (as depicted).

DECORATIVE FINISHES

CEMENT

In its natural state, cement is not very attractive, and paving or tiling over it can be costly. Luckily, there are ways of beautifying bare concrete floors. Existing and new floors can be decorated to simulate various finishes, such as terra-cotta tiles or paving stones, both of which are effective ways of enhancing an otherwise plain floor.

FLOORS

Surface Preparation

Concrete floors must be scrubbed with a wire brush to remove loose paint, and washed with TSP (trisodium phosphate) and warm water to remove grease. Use a suitable solvent to remove any sticky glue left after lifting old tiles or linoleum, then wash the area with TSP.

Trying to fill small holes or smooth an uneven surface is problematic and not always successful. If the surface is very bad you may have to re-skim with new concrete, or you can leave the floor as it is for added character.

Before the floor is painted, apply a suitable undercoat, followed by two coats of the appropriate base color.

Modern water-based paints are of such a high quality that they are durable enough to use on floors. However it is advisable to apply three to four coats of acrylic or polyurethane varnish to protect the finish.

Concrete floors can be effectively decorated with either flat color or innovative paint techniques.

Stenciled Mosaics and Borders

MATERIALS

- Water-based emulsion paint in three or four colors of your choice (including a base color)
- Artists' acrylic paint for small areas
- Universal tints
- Acrylic scumble glaze
- Water
- Water-based gloss varnish

EQUIPMENT

- 3 or 4 containers for mixing paints
- Brushes: thin artists' brushes; varnish brush; stencil brush or swab (see pg 60); flat 1" (25mm) nylon brush
- Foil plates for blending colors
- Paper towel
- Craft knife for cutting stencils
- Stencil card or acetate
- Tracing paper and carbon paper
- Chalk line
- Measuring tape
- Set square
- Cutting mat or thick sheet of glass
- Graph paper and pencil
- Masking tape
- Rags
- Protective latex gloves
- Plastic or cloth drop cloths to protect surfaces

Read the section on stencils (pg 54) before attempting this technique.

Patio and terrace floors can be transformed by a stenciled pattern. Stenciling is much quicker than trying to achieve the same effect by painting, and is equally suited to random and geometric designs. The size of the pattern should be in proportion to the size of the floor (for example, do not use large motifs in a small area).

Planning the Floor

Measure the length and width of the floor space you wish to paint. Establish the center point of the area by dividing the length and width in half. Mark these points by stretching a chalk line between the halfway marks (two people are needed to do this). Lift the line up and snap it down to leave a chalk line on the floor.

Drawing the floor plan to scale on graph paper will enable you to determine the pattern size and the placement of tiles, borders, etc. Trace the pattern outline onto the scaled-down floor plan. Then draw a grid (usually a scale of 1:20) on tracing paper and place it over the floor plan. From the reduced grid on the floor plan, scale up a proportionately bigger grid on the actual floor area on which you want to paint the design. Mark the bigger grid by snapping the chalk line between the opposite points until the entire grid is marked out on the floor. Check the right angles with a set square. If you want tiles on the diagonal, lines can be drawn to create the effect of diamond shapes. When the grid is accurate, copy an enlarged design to correspond to the scaled-down version on the tracing paper.

For tile floors, divide the length and width to see how many tiles will fit into the design. For example, nine 12" × 12" (30 x 30cm) tiles will cover an area of 3 sq. yds. (2.7m²).

Stenciling Mosaics

Stenciling is ideal for replicating mosaics in a border or as a pattern around a decorative object on a floor or wall. Mosaics are either small square chips of commercially produced ceramic or glass tiles, or existing tiles chopped up into irregular shapes. Sheets of ready prepared mosaic are usually 12" × 12" (30 × 30cm) square, so if you are doing large areas, it is more authentic to use this option.

TECHNIQUE

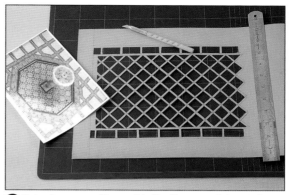

1 Draw mosaic squares, ¾" × ¾" (15 × 15mm), onto graph paper, leaving ⅛" (3mm) gaps between each piece. Leave a border of 2" (5cm) around the stencil to catch paint that spreads over the edges. Using carbon paper, transfer the drawing to the stencil card.

2 Cut out squares with a craft knife. Glass mosaic is not always symmetrical, so cuts do not have to be absolutely regular and can be done without a ruler.

3 Mix two or three colors of a similar tone. Adding acrylic scumble glaze and more water to the paint mixture makes it more transparent, resulting in a glassy look.

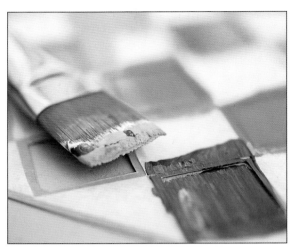

4 Mask off the tiles you want to leave white or paint a different color. Dip the stencil brush into one of the selected colors and dab off the excess paint on a paper towel. Use circular movements to rub each color alternately through the unmasked squares to create the variations that occur in mosaic. The stencil brush should not have too much paint on it.

5 Glass mosaic is not a flat color and to create a glassy effect, dip the tip of the flat nylon paintbrush into a few colors alternately and streak them lightly into each other.

6 Remove the masking tape and carefully paint in the white tiles using a flat nylon brush. Touch up any smudges, using a small artists' brush dipped into the base color, which now represents the grout. Varnish with water-based gloss varnish.

Stenciling a Border Pattern

Very simple geometric or random border designs can enhance existing or new cement floors. Borders can also be painted or stenciled onto existing tiles. If the area is not symmetrical, leave a wide plain border around the design, as this visually eliminates any irregularities.

TECHNIQUE

1 If working on a tiled floor, position the stencil on an existing tile. Line up the edges and mark them. These are the registration lines. If the floor is not tiled, mark out the position of the border with a chalk lines.

2 Determine which two (or more) colors you want to use. With masking tape, mask off the area to be covered by the second color.

3 Having lined up the edges, stick the stencil into position using masking tape. Apply the first color. Continue applying the first color to every alternate tile. When dry, repeat on the remaining tiles.

4 Remove the masking tape from the second color and tape up the first color. Stencil in the second color.

Painted Tiles and Borders

MATERIALS
- Water-based emulsion: in terra-cotta, ochre, or colors of your choice
- Artists' acrylic paint
- Water-based matte floor varnish
- Water

EQUIPMENT
- Chalk line
- Set square
- Tracing paper
- Paper and pencil
- Masking tape ½" (12mm)
- 2" (50mm) paintbrush and/or smaller
- Sea sponge
- Felt-tip marker
- Protective latex gloves
- Plastic or cloth drop cloths to protect surfaces

Painted Tiles

Faux tiles, borders, and any other designs can be painted directly onto the floor. Follow the procedure described on page 72 to determine where the pattern should be placed. Tiles make very effective baseboards or borders, particularly blue and white Dutch-style tiles painted in naive or primitive designs.

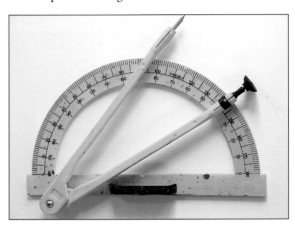

TECHNIQUE

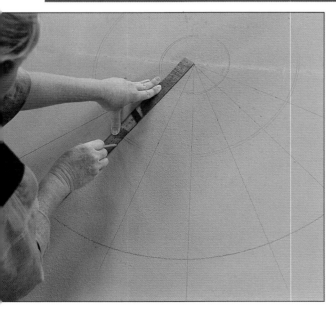

1 Follow the steps for planning the floor (see page 72). Paint the floor with a base coat in the color you want the grouting (the space between the tiles) to be. For example, terra-cotta tiles traditionally have a pale cement-gray grouting.

2 Draw the plan onto the floor, scaled up from your design. Use a chalk line to get your starting point or to find the center of the area that is to be painted.

3 For painted tiles, stick ½" (12mm) masking tape down one side of the chalk lines to indicate the grouting between the tiles. Complete this over the entire area. Rub the masking tape down well or else the paint will seep underneath it and smudge. For a narrower grout, use thin plastic tape of the type used in auto body shops.

4 For large, solid color tiles, use a 2" (50mm) brush and paint from the edges toward the center to avoid bleeding under the masking tape. Use a smaller brush for smaller tiles.

5 A damp sponge can be dipped into the paint mixtures and sponged onto the tile to add more texture. Two or three similar colors that are close in tone can be used to give the tiles a realistic stone, marble, or terra-cotta appearance.

6 When the paint is dry, remove the masking tape, pulling it off at an angle close to the surface.

7 Touch up any marks on the grout by painting them with the base coat. Finish off by sealing the floor with a good waterproof varnish, which should always be used to protect outdoor paint.

MATERIALS
- Water-based emulsion paint: in black, pearly white
- Water-based matte varnish

EQUIPMENT
- Flat nylon paintbrush 1" (25mm)
- Graph paper and pencil
- Tape measure
- Chalk line
- Low-tack tape
- Craft knife
- Thin cardboard template
- Water-soluble crayon
- Roller
- Paint tray and plastic bag
- Protective latex gloves

Painted Borders

TECHNIQUE

1 Choose a suitable design and decide what colors you want to use.

2 Measure the floor and draw your design to scale on graph paper.

3 Superimpose the border onto the floor plan, positioning it so that it is equidistant from the walls. Decide on the width (which must be proportionate to the size of the floor). If necessary, a border can be slightly further from one wall than another to accommodate the pattern. In this example, the border consists of a geometric diamond grid of tiles with rectangular tiles on either side; therefore, you need extremely accurate measurements to ensure that the pattern fits into the available floor space.

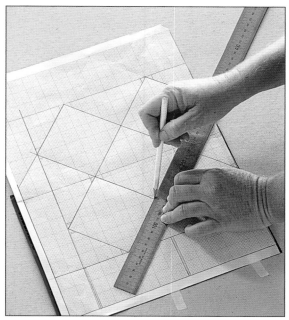

4 Draw the pattern up to full scale on graph paper. Make a template by transferring the full-scale pattern onto thin cardboard and cut it out with a craft knife, leaving bridges to hold the diamonds together.

5 Paint the floor with two coats of water-based emulsion paint. Mix a small amount of black water-based emulsion with white to make a pale gray color, imitating tile grout. Leave 24 hours drying time between coats.

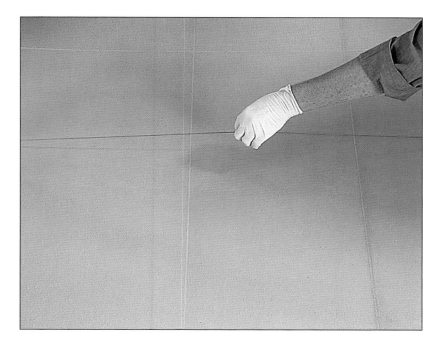

6 Use a tape measure to determine the position of the border on the floor. Mark the outside and inside edges on the floor with a chalk line.

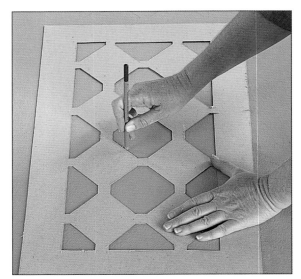

7 Position the template between the chalk lines on the floor and trace through the cut out sections with a water-soluble crayon.

9 Paint all the black diamond tiles first, painting from the outside of the diamond toward the center.

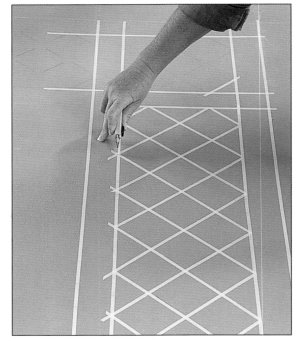

8 Mark off the tiles by placing low tack tape over the drawn lines to mark the "grouting" lines. Use a craft knife to cut the tape neatly at the corners. Rub the tape down well.

10 When thoroughly dry, carefully paint in all the white tiles without going over the edges of the masking tape.

11 When dry, remove all the tape. If paint has seeped under the tape, touch up with an artists' brush and some base coat. Finish with two coats of good matte floor varnish.

DECORATIVE FINISHES

WOOD

Wood is used for doors, porches, decks, fences, trellises, furniture, planters, and other items. It can be stained, varnished, painted, or left in its raw state to weather naturally. Once wood has been treated with a finish of any kind, it needs to be regularly maintained, allowing you to try out various techniques over time.

FINISHES

Surface Preparation

It is not always necessary to go to the extent of a decorative paint finish to give wooden surfaces a new lease on life. Often a good coat of fresh paint in a new color can do the decorating trick and give an outdoor area or the exterior of a home a new look.

The rule for a well-painted finish is to pay careful attention to surface preparation. Any uneven or rough spots will show up on a flat painted surface. It is advisable to use oil-based paint on exterior woodwork as this is more durable and will stand up to weathering. Choose an oil-based paint with either a high gloss or satin sheen finish.

Raw Wood

Cover each knot in the wood with two coats of shellac or commercial knotting to prevent resin from seeping out and staining the painted surface. Both products should be available at your local hardware store. Next, apply a coat of pink or white oil-based wood primer. The oil penetrates the surface, creating a protective layer. When dry, lightly sand, and apply universal undercoat.

Pre-Painted Woodwork in Good Condition

Give the surface a wash with TSP to remove any grease. Fill small cracks or nail holes with commercial wood filler and sand when dry. Always sand the entire surface regardless of the type of paint to be used. A good key is needed on woodwork to allow new layers of paint to adhere well.

Pre-Painted Woodwork in Poor Condition

Try to avoid complete paint removal, as this is a very time-consuming and messy operation. Rather, peel off loose paint or varnish with a scraper, trying not to damage the wood, and fill holes and large cracks with wood filler. Sand the surface with different grades of sandpaper, ending with the finest grade. If large areas of paint remain, try to sand the edges to make them less visible when top coating. If you choose the paint removal route, use an electric heat gun as it is less messy and less toxic than liquid stripper. You could also take the item to a professional paint stripping company.

Once the surface is prepared (repaired or completely stripped, washed, and sanded), follow the paint procedure for raw wood.

These stylish Versailles planters complement the earthy tones of the surrounding garden.

A variety of decorative finishes can be used to make wooden doors and windows a focal point.

Flat Paint

MATERIALS

- Paint stripper (if necessary—see surface preparation on pg 74)
- Pink or white oil-based wood primer
- Oil-based enamel or milk paint in the color of your choice
- Mineral spirits
- TSP
- Water

EQUIPMENT

- Flat decorators' brushes in sizes 2" and 1" (50 and 25mm)
- Scraper
- Sandpaper (various grades)
- Bucket and scrubbing brush to wash the surface
- Masking tape
- Protective latex gloves
- Plastic or cloth drop cloths to protect surfaces

There has been a renewed interest in traditional painting materials such as milk (or casein) paint, which was used extensively on woodwork and wooden furniture in Scandinavia and colonial America. The separated curds from soured skim milk were washed, dried, ground into powder, and then added to slaked lime. This produced a very strong water-based paint that, when completely dry, was totally water resistant and had a soft satin sheen finish. Its lime content also made it a disinfectant and it protected woodwork from borer beetles. Some paint companies have started to manufacture casein paint again and it is worth looking for it if you want to create an authentic old-country look.

Use the correct painting technique to achieve a smooth finish on wood.

TECHNIQUE

2 Load the brush and lay the paint on in vertical strokes.

1 Follow the appropriate surface preparation required. (Read the manufacturer's instructions if you are using milk paint—most do not require primer or undercoat.) Cover hinges, handles, keyholes, etc., with masking tape. If working with a brush, it is best to paint large flat areas in small sections, starting at the top and working down. Dip the tip of the bristles into the paint and wipe off the excess on the edge of the can. Never overload the brush with paint or submerge the bristles deeper than the ferrule.

3 Without reloading, paint horizontally across the vertical strokes to spread the paint evenly.

4 Always finish off each section with light, vertical strokes to eliminate brush marks. Reload the brush and paint the next section.

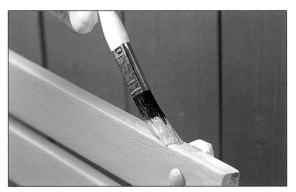

5 When painting narrow areas, use a small brush and always work over a section with a second or third stroke to avoid drips forming on the surface.

Bleaching or Liming

MATERIALS

- White liming wax
- Clear wax furniture polish and whiting (white pigment powder)
- White water-based emulsion paint
- Universal tints in raw umber
- Spirit wood stain in a dark color (optional)
- Water-based varnish
- Matte or satin varnish
- Mineral spirits
- TSP
- Water

EQUIPMENT

- Brushes: flat decorators' brush 2" (50mm); wire brush; varnish brush
- Sandpaper and fine steel wool
- Flat spatula or spackle tool
- Containers for paint and water
- Clean cloths or rags
- Protective latex gloves
- Plastic or cloth drop cloths to protect surfaces

Bleaching or limewashing (liming) wood is a very effective means of whitening the surface of outdoor furniture, doors, and wooden beams. The finish can be achieved by different methods. This section shows how to use water-based paint or liming wax instead of acid to bleach wood. Oak is traditionally used for limewashing because it has an open grain, which takes the whitening process.

Surface Preparation

1 Ideally, wood should be stripped of all hard varnish and stain, washed with a strong solution of TSP, then rinsed with water.

2 Brush oak and other soft woods firmly with a wire brush to open up the grain, always brushing in the direction of the grain. Pine is not open grained, but by using force, one can make scratches with a wire brush. The paint will then stick in the grooves.

3 Alternatively, sand the piece well to get a key for the liming paint.

Liming with Wax

TECHNIQUE

1 Brush on the liming wax with a stiff brush. Liming wax can be bought, or it can be made by adding white pigment powder to clear wax furniture polish. As it is semi-transparent it allows the grain of the wood to show through.

2 With a clean cloth, rub the wet wax into the grooves, using a circular movement.

3 Wet a soft cloth with mineral spirits and lightly wipe off the surplus wax. Follow the grain, but be careful not to remove the wax from it. The purpose is to get an even spread of wax.

4 Allow the wax to dry, then buff with a soft cloth to obtain a satin sheen finish.

Liming with Paint

2 When working with water-based paint on raw wood, first apply a very diluted coat of water-based varnish (about 5:1) to seal the wood, otherwise the paint immediately soaks into the wood, leaving a white blob. If previously varnished, sand well.

1 Dilute white water-based emulsion with water to the required strength, testing on a piece of scrap wood. Add a few drops of universal tint to soften or antique the white (raw umber gives a greenish brown tinge; raw sienna a slightly yellow look).

Tip *Some light woods, such as pine, tend to reflect a pink color when washed with white, and it is advisable to add a few drops of the complementary color (green) into the white to neutralize the pink. Alternatively, first stain the wood with a teak or dark oak spirit wood stain, and then seal it as in step 2.*

3 Apply the paint to the surface with a paintbrush and allow it to set for about five minutes. Have a cloth pad or steel wool handy to wipe off excess paint until the grain of the wood shows through.

4 The easiest way to apply paint to flat surfaces without heavy smudges is to cover the flat spatula or spackle tool with a double layer of fine T-shirt material, then dip it into the paint mixture and pull it down the wood, parallel to the grain. This is particularly effective on smooth wood such as previously varnished and sanded pine, as it results in a slightly striated finish.

5 Allow to dry overnight, then sandpaper lightly and finish with one or two coats of matte or satin varnish.

White walls, simple furniture, and limewashed wood contribute an air of informality to this beachfront home.

Distressing Wood

SHOPPING LIST

MATERIALS
- Wood stain in your chosen color
- Water-based emulsion paint in your chosen color
- Denatured alcohol/methylated spirits
- Artists' acrylic paint: in raw umber, black
- Matte water-based varnish
- Acrylic scumble glaze
- Mineral spirits
- Petroleum jelly
- Wax candle
- Rottenstone or clay powder

EQUIPMENT
- Separate containers for paint, water, solvents, antiquing mix
- Brushes: 2" and ¾" (50 and 15mm) paintbrushes; stiff bristle brush
- Tools for distressing: rasp, file, link-chain, sharp rocks, round-headed hammer, small wood drill
- Sandpaper
- Scraper
- Cloths
- Steel wool
- Protective latex gloves
- Plastic drop or cloth drop cloths to protect surfaces

Distressing is the simulation of signs of age such as wormholes, scratches, peeling, chipped, and worn paint. The effects of long use, weathering, and the wear and tear that occur naturally on old pieces of furniture, doors, and other objects can be recreated easily. The techniques described here can be applied to both old and new wood.

TECHNIQUE

1 If the wood is new, stain it with a dark or rich-colored spirit wood stain so that it acquires the appearance of age. Dilute the stain 50:50 with denatured alcohol. If it is too light, apply another coat.

2 To simulate chipped paint, dab on petroleum jelly in patches then elongate with your finger in the direction of the wood grain. Only do this on edges and sections where paint would have chipped off naturally.

3 To get the look of worn paint, rub a wax candle over the areas where you want more of the base coat to show through.

4 Paint water-based emulsion over the entire piece, gently covering the petroleum jelly and candle wax.

5 When the paint is thoroughly dry, remove the wax and petroleum jelly with the scraper or a cloth dipped in mineral spirits, which is a solvent.

6 To simulate several layers of paint, a second working of petroleum jelly can be applied and a completely different color added for an even more aged look. Again, remove the excess with a scraper and wipe with a cloth and mineral spirits.

7 Various implements can be used to physically distress objects to age them. Use a rasp or file to blunt corners and edges, or hit the object with a heavy chain to make indentations. A sharp stone can make deep gouges and scratches, and a round-headed hammer can flatten protrusions or dent moldings, which can be smoothed afterwards with sandpaper. Wormholes can be simulated with a very small drill. These can be clustered, single, or adjacent but should never be evenly spaced.

Antiquing Glaze

Mix raw umber with a small amount of black artists' acrylic color and a little water to make a thick, creamy mixture, then add acrylic scumble glaze or water-based varnish for transparency. If the mixture is too dark, add more scumble glaze. The leftover mixture can be stored in a container for other projects.

TECHNIQUE

1 Dab a few brush strokes of the mixture onto the object, using a stiff brush to work the glaze into all the cracks and indentations.

2 Spread the glaze with a soft cloth. Allow it to set for 15 to 30 minutes.

3 Wipe off the mixture, using a cloth or steel wool to accentuate the highlights. Leave more in cracks where dirt would have collected. If the glaze dries too quickly, wet the cloth with denatured alcohol.

4 To get an older dusty look, dip a stiff bristle brush into dry clay powder or rottenstone. Shake off the excess and dab it into the wet glaze.

Fading and peeling paint, dents, and cracks are the result of years of weathering—or is it artistic flair?

DECORATIVE FINISHES

FAUX METAL

Country gardens increasingly include rusted furniture and decorative items that show more artful decay than historic value. The natural way to obtain these finishes is to expose items to the elements and employ a great deal of patience. However, faux metal finishes are more easily achieved with paint or by applying metal leaf.

FiNiSHES

Surface Preparation

When deciding on a metal finish, keep in mind the effects of natural decay, and apply the appropriate finish to the item. For example, an old watering can will look more authentic with a rust finish than with a pewter or verdigris finish. Faux metal finishes can be applied to any material provided the surface is smooth and does not have a distinct grain. Rough terracotta or cement are not appropriate, but most metal finishes will work on metal, plastic, wood, or plaster.

Metal

Ensure that the surface is free of any rust or loose paint by rubbing it down with sandpaper or steel wool. Use a cloth to remove the dust. Apply a coat of rustproof paint, followed by a coat of metal primer. The item can then be painted with any type of paint.

Plastic

Wash the surface first with denatured alcohol to remove grease, then wash it with a strong detergent. Roughen the surface with fine sandpaper and then wipe it with acetone. Apply universal undercoat or a plastic primer (if one is available) and follow with two layers of base coat.

Wood

The best wooden surfaces for metal finishes are items made in a superwood or composite wood that has no natural grain. It is preferable that the item is new and does not need to have any old paint removed from it. Ensure the surface is clean and free of any dust and then apply a coat of pink or white oil-based wood primer. The oil penetrates the surface, creating a protective layer. When dry, sand lightly and apply a coat of universal undercoat.

Plaster

Smooth, newly plastered surfaces are ideal and only need dusting down before applying a coat of plaster primer or appropriate sealer (ask your paint dealer to recommend one, as these differ from one manufacturer to the next). When dry, apply universal undercoat, followed by the required base coat.

Time has weathered this metal clock.

Metal planters in a tranquil garden show the attractive effects that result from natural weathering.

Metal Leaf

MATERIALS
- Book of metal leaf of your choice
- Oil- or water-based paint for the base coat (traditional base colors for gold leaf are mustard yellow or dark red terra-cotta)
- Oil- or water-based gold size
- Metallic powder
- Oil- or water-based varnish

EQUIPMENT
- Brushes: flat nylon brushes 1¼" and ¾" (30 and 15mm); flat varnish brush 2" (50mm); Japanese hake; stiff round bristle brush
- Sandpaper
- Scissors
- Soft cloth
- Protective mask
- Protective latex gloves
- Plastic or cloth drop cloths to protect surfaces

There are five kinds of metal leaf: gold, silver, aluminum, copper, and brass (also known as Dutch metal or Dutch gold). These can be used to enhance decorative details on garden furniture, such as wrought iron chairs and tables, and various other items. Traditionally, old black cast iron railings were always embellished with gilding. London's Buckingham Palace is a classic example where details on the gates and railings have been decorated with real gold leaf. Gold and aluminum leaf do not tarnish, unlike brass, silver, and copper leaf, all of which have to be protected by a coat of varnish or shellac.

Metal leaf is available either loose or as transfer leaf, both of which come in book form. Loose leaf is interleaved with rouge paper, and transfer leaf is usually attached to a waxed paper backing. The leaves are extremely thin and very easily torn, as they are only ¹⁄₂₅₀,₀₀₀" (0.0001mm) thick. Since loose leaf blows away easily and is very difficult to work with, we suggest using only transfer leaf.

Metal leaf is normally applied to an object over a tacky layer of size (an adhesive varnish with a drying time of 1 to 12 hours that is used to hold down metal leaf). For items that are to be exposed to weather, use oil-based gold size. Milky water-based size, which is clear when dry, is preferred for objects that are kept under cover, such as on a covered patio.

Metallic powders come in many colors, such as rich gold, pale gold, and various bronze powders. They can be mixed with varnish and painted onto an area, or dusted into indentations. Alternatively, the object can be painted with an oil-based gold size and the metallic powder dusted on. When using metallic powders, always cover your mouth and nose with a mask and wear eye protection.

TECHNIQUE

1 See that the object is dust free and as smooth as possible. Paint the object with the desired base coat color and allow to dry for 24 hours.

2 Sand the object lightly with fine (400-grit) sandpaper to remove any imperfections.

3 Using a large flat nylon brush, paint the entire object with oil- or water-based size. Use even strokes and try not to go over any areas a second time, particularly when using water-based size, as it tends to become rubbery.

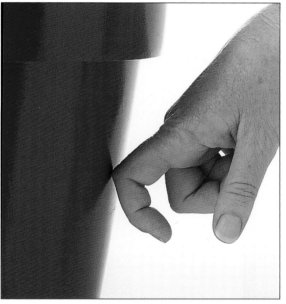

4 Wait until the size becomes tacky (test by touching it with your knuckle). The "open-time" of size is the period during which you are able to stick the metal leaf to it before it dries completely.

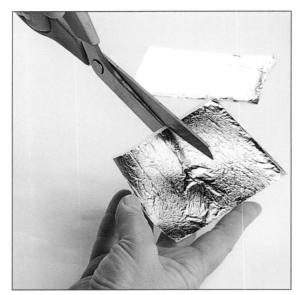

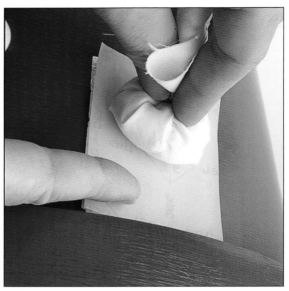

5 Cut the sheet of transfer metal leaf into four strips or quarters, as it is much easier to work with smaller pieces.

6 Take the leaf to the project by holding the paper backing. Avoid touching the leaf as it will tarnish. First stick one edge of the metal leaf onto the sized article, then dab down the whole piece with a soft cloth. Lift off the backing paper.

7 Overlap the next piece slightly and continue until the object is completely covered. Use a soft cloth to rub down the leaf quite firmly to smooth out the wrinkles.

8 Take a soft paintbrush (such as a Japanese hake) and brush down the seams with short jabbing movements. This will remove the excess leaf and leave a clean join.

9 If there are any grooves or indentations in the object, take a dry stiff bristle brush, dip it into the metallic powder and dab it onto the sticky glaze in the hollows.

10 The final step is to varnish the object using a water-based varnish (if it is to remain under cover) or oil-based polyurethane varnish (if it is outdoors). Avoid using varnish in humid or damp weather.

Tip *Loose metal leaf can be easily handled in the following manner: adhesive labels come attached to paper that is shiny on one side. Remove the labels and carefully place the sheet, shiny side down, on top of the loose leaf. Rub it down well. It then becomes transfer leaf. Kitchen wax paper can be used in the same manner.*

This gold leaf pot, created by French artist Jean-Pierre Raynaud, makes a dramatic focal point in his garden.

Verdigris

SHOPPING LIST

MATERIALS

- Water-based emulsion for the base coat: in copper, gray, dark green, black
- Paint: three or four ready-mixed water-based emulsion colors, which will remain constant regardless of the base color
- Universal tints or acrylics: in blue, green, raw umber, black, white
- Matte oil-based varnish
- Filler paste to add texture to colors (optional)
- Gray chalk powder, clay dust, or rottenstone

EQUIPMENT

- 2 or 3 natural sea sponges
- A bucket of water to dampen sponges
- 4 small containers for paints
- Brushes: varnish brush; decorators' brushes: 2" and 1" (50 and 25mm)
- Protective latex gloves
- Plastic or cloth drop cloths to protect surfaces

Tip #1 *Remember to apply the green and blue paint colors randomly to achieve a more natural look.*

Verdigris is a green-turquoise, chalky patina that appears when copper, brass, or bronze becomes weathered. It is an attractive aged finish that is easy to achieve on various garden ornaments and objects, including furniture, old copper lamps, garden pots, and even plastic chairs and containers, all of which can be disguised and transformed by using this finish.

In order to see the real color of verdigris, paint any copper object with ordinary household bleach and after a couple of days it will become turquoise. The object can be restored to its original color and shine by polishing.

TECHNIQUE

1 Apply the copper paint for the base coat. Paint large areas with a 2" (50mm) brush and small areas with a 1" (25mm) brush. Allow the base coat to dry.

2 Select three or four colors that will be used to obtain the verdigris effect (white with a combination of universal tints in dark turquoise, light turquoise, dark green, or putty gray), and dirty each color with a little raw umber or black tint. This can also be done with artists' acrylic paint.

Tip #2 *As an optional base coat, either metal leaf (preferably copper) or gray, black, or dark green water-based emulsion can be applied to the surface.*

3 If a crumbly effect is desired, mix the colors with filler paste.

4 Soak the sea sponges in water and squeeze out the excess. Dip a sponge into the darkest color first (dark green or dark turquoise) and sponge randomly onto the object with light pouncing movements. Do not cover the base coat completely.

5 Sponge on the second and third colors, which will be lighter than the first. While the paint is still wet, blend the colors together.

6 Sponge the lightest color onto the raised areas.

7 Squeeze a sponge soaked with diluted paint over the object to simulate streaks made by rain on flat surfaces.

8 Verdigris items are never shiny, so when the paint dries, apply clear matte (not gloss) varnish for protection.

9 Before the varnish is fully dry, dust chalk, clay dust powder, or rottenstone into hollows and indentations.

This stylized tableau is actually a metal sculpture that has weathered to a perfect verdigris finish.

Rust

MATERIALS
- Black and white water-based emulsion paint
- Artists' acrylic paint: in raw sienna, burnt sienna, burnt umber, red oxide
- Ultramarine universal tint
- Fine builders' sand

EQUIPMENT
- Containers for mixing paints
- Brushes: 1" (25mm) decorators' fitch; No. 5 artists' brush
- Protective latex gloves
- Plastic or cloth drop cloths to protect surfaces

This metal finish is often regarded as a problem when it occurs naturally. However, a look of age and decay is now very fashionable. Any metal piece that has not been treated with a rust-proofing agent could start rusting within one rainy season, which is one way to get this finish without any effort. However, the natural way normally takes a bit more time, so we have described a quick and easy way to create faux rust on any surface using water-based paint.

TECHNIQUE

1 In a container, mix black emulsion with small amounts of white and ultramarine to make a dark charcoal base coat. Paint the prepared surface.

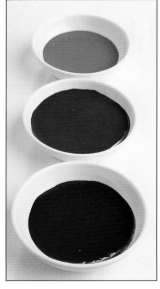

2 Using artists' acrylics, mix two-thirds burnt sienna and one-third burnt umber in a container to make a good dark brown rust color. Mix burnt sienna, red oxide, and burnt umber in another container to make a light reddish brown rust color. In a third container, mix raw sienna with a drop of red oxide to make a yellow rust color.

3 Using the 1" (25mm) fitch, stipple the dark brown rust color over the surface, allowing the base coat to show in places. To achieve the pitted texture of rust, sprinkle fine, sifted builders' sand onto the wet paint and work it in with a brush.

4 Repeat this process with the reddish brown rust color, still allowing the other colors to show through. The stippling action of the brush will further enhance the grainy sand finish.

5 Using a fine artists' brush, paint the third (yellow rust) color into the fine details of the molding. This color will occur where rainwater would normally collect and puddle.

Plump, glossy succulents contrast with the desiccated finish of this rusted urn.

Lead

MATERIALS

- Water-based emulsion paint: in black, white
- Ultramarine universal tint
- Rottenstone or pale gray tile grout
- Water-based varnish

EQUIPMENT

- Containers for mixing colors
- Sea sponge
- Brushes: varnish brush; bristle fitch; 2" and ¾" (50 and 15mm) decorators' brushes
- Protective latex gloves
- Plastic or cloth drop cloths to protect surfaces

Real lead takes on a lovely dull blue-gray patina when exposed to rain. This can easily be recreated with emulsion paint to elegantly transform any garden accessory, from planters and window boxes to furniture and architectural details like weather vanes and fountains. The effect is similar in appearance to wrought iron, a popular material that is often used for garden furniture and decorative items such as Victorian plant stands and balustrades.

TECHNIQUE

1 Mix a dark blue-gray base coat by adding some white emulsion and a few drops of ultramarine universal tint to black emulsion paint.

2 Using a 2" (50mm) decorators' brush, apply the base coat to the entire surface, then allow it to dry.

3 Pour some of the base color into a separate container and add more white to lighten the gray. Use a dampened sea sponge to wet small areas at a time. This slows the drying process and makes the paint applied in the next step more workable.

4 Use the ¾" (15mm) decorators' brush to paint the paler gray onto the raised dampened areas, highlighting them.

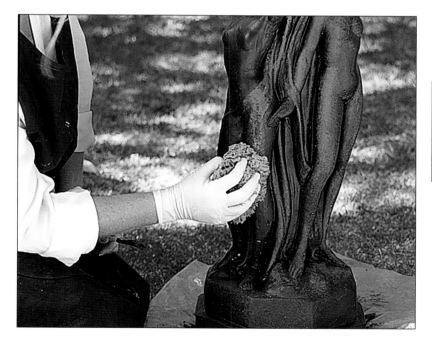

5 Use a damp sponge to further soften the highlighted areas.

Tip *Use a light hand when dabbing with the damp sponge to avoid adding too many highlights to the statue.*

6 Mix a very diluted pale gray water-based emulsion. Soak a sea sponge in the paint and squeeze it from the top, allowing the wash to run the natural course that rainwater would take, streaking the surface and collecting in the crevices.

7 Allow to dry; and then finish with two coats of acrylic matte varnish.

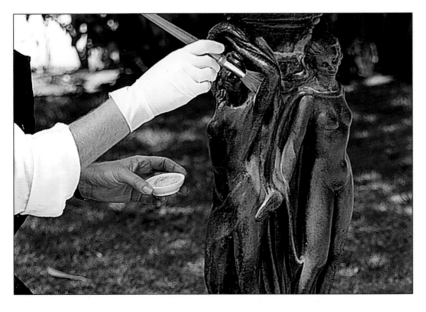

8 Before the varnish dries, dust on the rottenstone or tile grout with a bristle fitch, paying special attention to areas with intricate details.

A solarium provides a secluded setting for this leaded fountain.

DECORATIVE FINISHES

STONE

Stone ornamentation can have a dramatic effect and impart a sense of grandeur. Many historic homes still have beautiful stone walls, weathered by time and the elements. Nowadays, real stone is hard to come by and is very expensive, but with paint and creativity, your walls, floors, and garden furniture can be transformed into faux stone.

FINISHES

Surface Preparation

The stone finishes described in this chapter are suitable for smooth cement floors and items that have been pre-cast in cement or terra-cotta clay.

Most garden accessory stores or nurseries have a wide range of planters, fountains, furniture, and statues. When choosing the appropriate finish for the item you wish to paint, keep in mind that a marble finish looks most authentic on a smooth surface (such as clay, smooth plastered walls, or a well-prepared cement floor). The other finishes will work perfectly on any rough or smooth surface.

Whichever surface you choose, make sure that it is well-cleaned, grease-free, and primed correctly.

If the object has never been painted before, or is a newly plastered wall or cement floor, brush it down to get rid of any loose dirt, then prime it with an appropriate isolating layer such as a universal primer. (Although this is an oil-based primer, it can be used under both oil-based and water-based topcoats.)

If the object is newly painted, sand it lightly before applying a water-based primer. When the primer is dry, apply one or two coats of an appropriately colored base paint, either a water-based emulsion or an oil-based paint.

If the object has been painted before, sand it with coarse sandpaper to remove any flaking paint and provide a key for the surface, before giving it a coat of primer and base coat.

Stone statuary adds a gracious note to gardens.

Stone is the one of the oldest building materials, yet remains an important architectural and design element.

Rough Granite

MATERIALS
- **Base coat**: white and black water-based emulsion; universal tints in raw umber and black
- **Granite finish**: universal tints in yellow oxide, raw umber, green, and black; denatured alcohol/methylated spirits; acrylic scumble glaze; artists' acrylic in white and black

EQUIPMENT
- Medium containers to mix colors
- Small containers
- Mixing plate
- 3 or 4 sea sponges
- Brushes: 2" (50mm) decorators' paintbrush; No. 4 and 8 artists' brushes; artists' fitches
- Bucket of water
- Brown paper
- Protective latex gloves
- Plastic or cloth drop cloths to protect surfaces

Granite, which is widely used for ornamentation, is found all over the world. Different countries produce distinctive varieties and colors ranging from pale gray to blue, greenish-gray, deep charcoal, and beautiful tones of pinks and terra-cotta, often covered with flashes of the vivid colors of lichen.

Creating a faux granite finish is a fairly simple process, which uses the basic techniques of sponging and spattering, with the added effect of solvent release. Before you start, look at real pieces of granite to decide what colors to use and to help you determine how much of each color to apply.

TECHNIQUE

1 For the base coat, pour some white water-based emulsion into a container and add a few drops of black and raw umber universal tints to tint the paint to a pale gray.

2 Apply two coats of base paint using the decorators' paintbrush, allowing the paint to dry for 24 hours between each coat.

3 Pour some white emulsion into separate containers and add tints to mix up four shades of gray, getting progressively darker. Add one-third acrylic scumble glaze to the two darker colors and dilute with one-third water to make a glaze.

Tip #1 *When doing a regular sponging technique on a wall, always use the same side of the sponge. However, for a granite effect, you can use all sides of the sponge to emulate the irregular marks of the stone.*

4 Soak three sea sponges in water and squeeze out the excess. Wearing gloves, start with the lightest color and dip a sponge into the paint. Cupping the sponge in your hand, test the pattern by dabbing it on a piece of brown paper. The pattern will either appear as a fine stipple effect or, by using the "brain" side of the sponge, a coarse and open pattern.

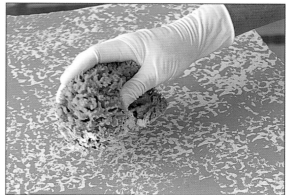

5 Using a definite but light dabbing movement, sponge over the entire object, changing the angle of the sponge with every five to six dabs. Dab randomly all over the surface, going back to fill in any big gaps but still allowing the base color to show through the pattern of the sponge.

6 Using a small artists' paintbrush, replicate the sponge markings in the indentations where the sponge can't reach.

7 Apply the next color in the same way as before, using the second damp sponge. While the second coat is still wet, use the remaining sponges to apply the third and fourth colors. Allow the last three colors to mix slightly in the sponging process.

Tip #2 *The size of the spatter depends on how hard you tap the stick and its distance above the surface. It is advisable to practice on a piece of brown paper before applying it to your finished article.*

8 Before the glazes begin to set, you should use your fingers to flick a little denatured alcohol onto the surface. This will cause the wet glaze to ciss (disperse into little craters) as the solvent begins to react with the paint.

9 Using artists' acrylic and enough water for a creamy consistency, mix black and white paint in separate containers. Load a fitch brush with white paint and dab off the excess. Standing over the object, tap the fitch against a stick or brush handle, so that flecks of paint spatter the surface. Repeat with black paint.

These granite creatures show the effects of years of guarding the portals of this chateau in the south of France.

Marble

MATERIALS
- White water-based emulsion paint
- Universal tints: in black, yellow ochre, raw umber
- Artists' acrylic: in black, white, raw umber, yellow ochre
- Acrylic scumble glaze
- Water-based varnish
- Denatured alcohol/methylated spirits
- Water

EQUIPMENT
- Plastic or foil plates for mixing colors
- 2 containers for mixing glaze
- Paper and pen
- Rags (at least one of fine T-shirt fabric)
- Fine sandpaper (400 grit)
- Brushes: Japanese hake or badger brush; stippling brush; No. 3 artists' round nylon or sable brush; 2" or 1" (50 or 25mm) decorators' brushes; flat bristle brush for spattering
- Optional materials to make marks: plastic film (cling film); blotting paper; feather (for veining)
- Protective latex gloves
- Plastic or cloth drop cloths to protect surfaces

Surface Preparation

Whether you are working on a flat surface, like a floor, or a decorative urn with molded areas, the surface should be as smooth as possible. Prepare the surface by using filler paste for small irregularities, then sandpaper well.

TECHNIQUE

1 Apply two coats of good-quality white acrylic emulsion paint as a base coat, allowing 24 hours drying time between coats.

Painted imitation marble is an amazing, inexpensive substitute for the real thing. Imitation marble has been found in ancient Egyptian tombs and grand European palaces, and is often so well executed that it is indistinguishable from real marble in appearance.

Marbling works well on walls and floors. Floor tiles, too, can be painted to simulate marble. Plastic or plaster reproductions cast from original works can also be successfully painted and antiqued to look like marble garden urns, columns, pots, pedestals, and statuary.

2 For the first glaze, mix equal proportions of white emulsion paint and acrylic scumble glaze with a few drops of universal tints. Thin this mixture with water to the consistency of very thin cream. For the second glaze (the shadow glaze), decant some white glaze into a container and add a few drops of black universal tint to create a darker gray color. An optional third shade can be created by adding raw sienna to white glaze in another container.

3 Fix a piece of paper over the object and use it to plan the marks that occur in marble, drawing in the shadows and cracks.

4 Apply the first coat of glaze to a section not larger than 12" × 12" (30 × 30cm) with jigsaw puzzle (irregular) edges, then go on to the next section.

5 Using the second, darker glaze, add a few shadows. These tend to follow one direction on the diagonal but do not run in visible stripes.

6 Using a stippling brush or cloth pad, work on the lightest areas first to eliminate brush strokes, then stipple the darker glaze, softly blending the two colors.

7 Use the artists' brush to add more dark shadows, then while the paint is still wet, use the stippler once again to merge the colors.

8 Soften with a Japanese hake or badger brush to smooth and polish (buff) the marble.

9 With a fine artists' brush and the light glaze, paint in veins and marks, then strengthen the color so the marks appear darker and thicker. They can also disappear into dark shadows. Soften again with a badger brush or Japanese hake.

Tip #1 *Before you begin using the marbling technique, it can be helpful to research images of real marble. This will allow you to not only choose the pattern and colors you want, but also realistically recreate the look of marble.*

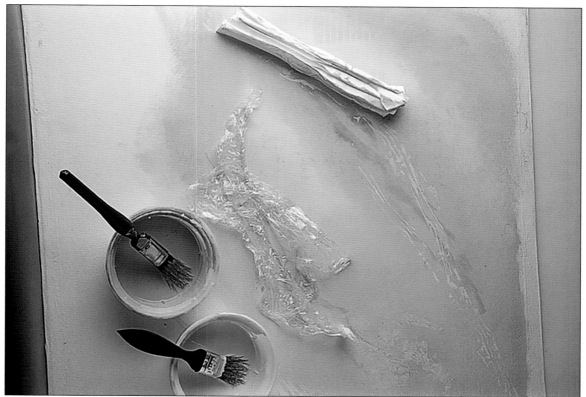

10 a) **Plastic film**: Drop a piece of crushed film onto the darkest area of the wet glaze and blow it down. Then lift it off. This pulls the glaze away and exposes the lighter base coat. Soften immediately. Crushing blotting paper and pressing it into the wet glaze creates the effect of crisp cracks.

b) **Solvent release**: A stiff, round bristle brush can be dipped into denatured alcohol. Using the brush, either carefully spatter the wet area or draw a thin line to simulate a light crack. As the solvent begins to eat into the glaze it will create interesting holes. The sponge can be dabbed onto the darker areas making larger craters, but it must not be too wet. All techniques must be softened, to make the marks appear as if they were in the marble.

11 A second working of smaller, delicate marks and finer cracks can be done with a fine artists' brush before varnishing.

12 Marble frequently has white striations running in opposite directions to the shadows and veining. You can achieve this effect by dipping a feather into white emulsion, blotting off the excess paint on a paper towel or plate, and then drawing the feather across the marble, lifting it at the end of each stroke to taper off the mark. Finish with two coats of water-based varnish leaving 24 hours drying time between each coat.

Tip #2 *If the marbling is too dark and the veins too definite, paint over with the first mixture of white glaze to soften the look before varnishing.*

Faux marbling must be done carefully and with attention to detail if it is to resemble the natural stone.

Antiqued and Weathered Cement

MATERIALS

- White water-based emulsion
- Universal tints: in raw umber, black
- Artists' acrylic paint: in black, white, raw umber, yellow ochre
- Acrylic scumble glaze
- Water
- Water-based matte varnish

EQUIPMENT

- Containers to mix colors
- Brushes: two 2" (50mm) decorators' brushes; flat artists' fitch; No. 4 and No. 8 artists' brushes
- Chamois
- Sandpaper
- Protective latex gloves
- Plastic or cloth drop cloths to protect surfaces

Tip #1 *To give your house a classical, Grecian or Roman look, consider using this technique on both columns and statues, then arrange them around a water feature in patterns similar to the image on page 131.*

If you are fortunate enough to have old pieces of sculpture standing in your garden or outdoor area, then this technique will not be required. However, most of us are not that lucky and have to resort to buying new pre-cast pieces from a nursery or garden accessory store. The following technique will enable you to turn your new acquisition into a beautifully antiqued piece that will look as if it has been outdoors forever.

TECHNIQUE

1 For the base coat, pour some of the white emulsion into two of the containers. Using a few drops each of black and raw umber universal tints, mix up two shades of stone, one slightly darker than the other. Using a different paintbrush for each color, paint the entire piece, using a chamois to blend the two colors. The finished base coat should have an uneven distribution of color with soft blending. Allow the base coat to dry. Keep the base coat colors for possible touching up.

2 Using the artists' acrylic paint, mix a few colors, ranging from dark charcoal or brown, sludgy green and dirty ochre, to grays a little darker than the base coat. Add one-third acrylic scumble glaze and a bit of water to make these mixtures the consistency of thin cream. Starting with the lightest color, use a clean decorator's brush and roughly paint into recesses, folds, and crevices, thinning the paint out in drifts over the molded areas. Build up the shadows, working from the lightest to the darkest shades. To decide where to place the color, imagine that you are dirtying the object and visualize where most of the dust and dirt would accumulate. Those will be the darkest areas. The raised areas would be more exposed to rain and have the least dirt. Do one area at a time so that the paint does not dry too quickly.

3 Take the dry, clean chamois and bunch it into your hand so that it has points and is not a smooth cushion. Lightly dab it over the painted areas to soften and blend the color. Do not rub or dab the surface too hard, as this will just remove the glaze entirely. Allow a short time for the glaze to set (it does not have to be totally dry).

4 Take a small quantity of the lightest base coat color and add some white water-based emulsion to lighten it even more. Take a flat fitch, load it with paint and wipe the excess off, leaving very little paint on the brush. Lightly run the brush over the raised areas to highlight them. Finish with two coats of water-based matte varnish if desired.

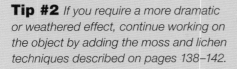

Tip #2 *If you require a more dramatic or weathered effect, continue working on the object by adding the moss and lichen techniques described on pages 138–142.*

This water feature weathered naturally but, with the correct materials, the effect can be artificially recreated.

Stone Blocking

SHOPPING LIST

MATERIALS
- Optional base coat: water-based emulsion paint (white tinted with raw umber or pale ivory)
- Artists' acrylic paint: in raw umber, white
- Universal tints: in black, brown, raw umber, yellow ochre, raw sienna (Alternatively, buy the same colors in ready-mixed water-based emulsion paint. Only small quantities are used to mix in with the white paint)
- Water-based filler-paste (optional)

EQUIPMENT
- 4 containers for paints
- Flat spatula to apply filler-paste
- 2 or 3 sea sponges or foam sponges
- Brushes: 4" and 2" (100 and 50mm)
- Bucket of water to dampen sponges
- Cardboard and cutting knife
- ⅛" (3mm) auto-body tape (to mask grouting between the stone blocks)
- Low-tack tape
- Paper
- Ruler or straight edge
- Level
- Set square
- Plumb line
- Coarse-grade (80 grit) sandpaper
- Water-soluble pencil
- Protective latex gloves
- Plastic or cloth drop cloths to protect surfaces

TECHNIQUE

The effect of dressed stone blocks with fine grout lines will enhance any featureless plaster wall, patio, or terrace. An authentic-looking textured stone effect can be achieved by applying water-based filler paste mixed with paint. The blocks can have beveled edges and dovetailing where they meet so that they look very three-dimensional. Colors should be subtle, as no two blocks of stone are identical.

1 Apply the color of your choice for the base coat. Use a 4" (100mm) brush to paint large areas and a 2" (50mm) brush for smaller areas. Allow to dry for 24 hours.

Marking out blocks: Measure the height and width of the area. Divide the height into equal-size blocks (the average size is 7" to 9" [200 to 230mm] high and 12" to 14" [300 to 350mm] wide).

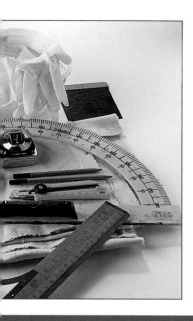

Tip #1 *This technique involves a lot of preplanning, so gather all of your supplies before you begin. Take your time as you measure out all of the lines; an uneven line will be very noticeable if you don't do it right.*

2 On a piece of paper, make a template of an alcove (attach the paper to the wall if necessary). Draw the radius and mark off the degrees to determine where the surrounding stone blocks will be placed.

3 Place the template in the alcove and mark off the measurements. Draw in the blocks with a water-soluble pencil.

4 For the vertical lines, fix the plumb line to the top of the wall with plastic putty or low-tack tape and let it hang down through the center mark. Place a set square against this line and draw in all the vertical and horizontal lines with pencil. A level can be used as a guide.

5 Stick the ⅛" (3mm) tape just below the horizontal lines and to one side of the vertical lines. Rub down the tape to prevent paint from seeping under it.

6 Cut a cardboard template the size of the block, leaving a margin of 4" (100mm) all around, because both the center section and the outer section will be used.

Tip #2 *Use a long ruler, rolling cutter, and cutting mat to easily measure and cut the straight lines needed for the cardboard templates.*

7 **Painting blocks**: Mix three or four similar tones by adding universal tints to white water-based emulsion paint. Dilute the mixtures with water to thin them down and increase the working time.

Tip #3 *Place your paint on a nearby, stable surface to avoid accidents as you work. Remember to place a drop sheet under your paint buckets to catch any paint that might drip.*

8 With the cardboard template, mask off the block you intend working on. Stick the template to the wall with low-tack tape or plastic putty. Paint the block with all the mixed colors, alternating them.

9 Use filler paste to obtain a rough texture on the blocks. This can either be mixed with the colors or applied first and then painted when dry. Pull a flat spatula across the wet paste, or build up texture by dabbing it, using a damp sponge.

10 Paint alternate blocks by brushing, sponging, or rubbing with a cloth. Paint the edges of the block first and then fill in the center. When these are dry, paint the adjacent blocks. It is best to leave the finish as pale as possible and darken some areas later if necessary.

11 Carefully remove the tape between the blocks. Marks made by water-soluble pencil can be removed with a damp sponge.

12 Make blocks look more three-dimensional by putting in shadows according to the light source, which normally comes from the top. Place a straightedge against one side of the block and use it as a guide for your hand. With a medium-sized brush, paint a lighter tone at the top of the block and on either the left or the right side (depending on the direction of the light). The bottom and opposite sides, where shadows are cast, will be darker. Use a dilute mixture of raw umber artists' acrylic paint for darker shadows and undiluted white for brighter shadows. Miter the corners where they join.

A stone-blocked wall and alcove create the perfect setting for a verdigris-finished wall decoration.

Moss and Lichen

MATERIALS

- **Moss**: Artists' acrylic in terre verte, raw umber, black, sap green, raw sienna
- **Lichen**: Artists' acrylic in sap green, ultramarine, white, raw umber
- Acrylic scumble glaze
- Water-based filler paste
- Water-based matte varnish

EQUIPMENT

- Brushes: 2 artists' fitches; 1" (25mm) decorators' paintbrush; varnish brush
- 2 to 3 small sea sponges
- Containers for mixing paint
- Nail brush and bucket of water
- Artists' palette knife
- Protective latex gloves
- Plastic or cloth drop cloths to protect surfaces

The beauty of recreating weather-beaten faux effects on outdoor objects is that they can be quite rough and haphazard. Real stone walls and ornamental objects that have been placed outdoors and exposed to the weather for many years have moss and lichen growing in the crevices and moldings, or where water naturally flows down the sides of the object. Colors can vary from the bright greens and sludgy olive shades of moss to the pale grays and limes found in lichen.

The effect of moss or lichen can be applied to any item already finished in a stone effect. It gives an authentic final touch to the granite finish described earlier in this chapter, as lichen grows profusely on natural granite. Moss effects can be applied to a column, fountain, planter, or statue finished in marble or sandstone.

> **Tip #1** *Since the colors of natural moss and lichen can vary, you will have more freedom in what your stone piece looks like. Choose a color within the natural range that matches your décor.*

Moss

TECHNIQUE

1 Look at the colors of real moss, then mix up three or four similar shades of green, ranging from a dark, sludgy green to vivid sap green.

2 Paint the object with the base color of your choice, then use a decorators' brush to add the first moss color, blending the two colors to create a dappled effect.

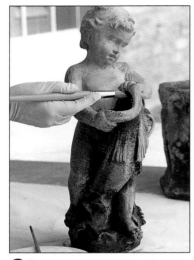

3 Concentrating on the areas where moss would naturally grow, use an artists' fitch to dab the other colors onto the surface and into the crevices. The edges of moss are subtle so blend the colors into each other. Allow the paint to dry.

4 While applying the colors, constantly blend and soften each area with a damp, clean sea sponge.

5 Apply small patches of the sap green paint. Using the artists' fitch, dip the brush into the paint and dab it onto the surface. Soften again with a damp sea sponge.

6 Allow the paint to dry thoroughly and then apply two coats of water-based matte varnish.

Moss covers an old stone statue.

Lichen

Lichen tends to occur on the weather side of objects and rarely covers them entirely. When doing this technique allow enough of the original surface to remain visible.

TECHNIQUE

1 Mix up a base color (this could be gray or a pale terra-cotta). Add filler paste to give the paint texture. If you are applying this technique to an object that has already been paint-finished in granite or terra-cotta, skip steps 1 and 2.

2 Using a decorator's paintbrush, apply the textured base coat with thick, uneven brush strokes, giving the surface more texture.

3 Having looked at the real colors of lichen, mix two to three shades of pale gray, dirty white, pale blue, lime green, and dark charcoal. Add a small amount of acrylic scumble glaze to each, plus a small amount of water-based filler paste to create texture.

4 Apply the colors alternately in patches, using an artist's palette knife. Some areas can be smoothed over while others can be layered with rough edges.

6 Apply the last and darkest color in the same way but in fewer places. These will be more prominent on the weather side of the object or where rainwater would flow and collect naturally.

5 While the paint is still wet, take a nail brush and stipple the rough paint surface in some areas. This action will help to blend the colors and leave a pitted texture, adding to the lichen effect.

The bold patches created by real moss and lichen are easily simulated with paint effects.

GALLERY

This traditional door from Bali demonstrates an excellent way to use flat paint on wood (see page 86) in order to add color and vivacity to an entranceway.

This distressed decorative wall pattern (see page 56) adds a unique beauty to the window here.

Rough granite planters (see page 118) lend a beautiful contrast to brightly colored flowers.

Adding a rusty, weather-beaten touch (see page 108) to decorative objects in your backyard will add warmth to your outdoor living space.

Using the verdigris technique (see page 104) on a sundial gives outdoor décor a more established, classical look.

Combining stone blocking (see page 132) and a stenciled mosaic (page 72) is an effective method of bringing a stone-faced wall or floor to life.

Consider blending a couple of the techniques from this book. Here, a simple white window border (page 56) and distressed green plaster paint (page 46) allow the warmth of the wooden window to pop.

Index

Polyurethane	Synthetic resin used on some paints and varnish.
Ragging	A technique that uses a crumpled rag to create decorative broken color finishes.
Size	An adhesive varnish with a drying time of between one and twelve hours, used to hold down metal leaf.
Skirting	A trim, usually of wood, between a wall and the floor.
Spackle	Ready mixed, all-purpose compound used for filling cracks or small holes in walls prior to painting.
Spattering	A painting technique in which a brush dipped in paint, glaze, or varnish is knocked to spray dots of color onto a surface.
Sponging	A painting technique that uses a damp sponge to create a dappled patchy effect.
Stippling	A technique used to soften and blend color, and eliminate brushstrokes.
Thixotropic	A term used to describe paint that returns to a gel state after mixing.
Tromp l'oeil	Painting which creates an optical illusion or "deceives the eye."
TSP	Trisodium phosphate, a concentrated, water-based cleanser that rinses clean without a residue.
Verdigris	The green color produced as a result of naturally occurring corrosion on copper, bronze, and brass.

Glossary

Acrylic	Water-based paint that becomes waterproof when dry.
Antiquing	Processes used to simulate natural ageing, wear, and tear.
Architrave	The molding around a doorway or window opening.
Bob	A ball of upholsterer's cotton wrapped in a square of silk and secured with a rubber band. Used to polish or smooth off fine paint surfaces.
Cissing	The effect created when solvent is spattered onto a painted surface that is still wet.
Color washing	Paint technique used to produce a softly textured, patchy finish, achieved by applying several layers of thin paint.
Dragging	Technique for pulling a long-haired brush through wet paint or glaze to produce a series of fine lines.
Drier	A medium, or additive, that thins paints and speeds drying time.
Glaze	Transparent or semi-transparent medium (oil- or water-based).
Grout	Thin mortar used to fill joints between tiles.
Knotting	A varnish used as a substitute for shellac.
Marbling	Variety of paint techniques designed to recreate artificially the appearance of marble.
Plumb line	A length of string with a weight tied to the bottom, used to obtain straight vertical lines down walls.

The mixture of fun, unique terra-cotta pot designs for the larger planters (see page 52) and smaller metal pots provides this potted garden variety and warmth.